D1064892

# THAT OUR CHILDREN
# MAY KNOW

# THAT OUR CHILDREN MAY KNOW

## Vanishing Wildlife in Zoo Portraits

by ROGER CARAS

and Sue Pressman

Longmeadow Press

Copyright © 1990 by Roger Caras

Copyright © 1990 by Donald Hutter Associates

Published by Longmeadow Press
201 High Ridge Road
Stamford, CT 06904

ISBN: 0-681-40598-8
Longmeadow Press edition first published 1991

All rights reserved. No part of this book may be reproduced or used in any
form or by any means, electronic or mechanical, including photocopying, recording, or by an information storage and retrieval system, without permission in writing from the publisher.

Designed by A. Christopher Simon

Printed in Hong Kong

0  9  8  7  6  5  4  3  2  1

*FOR DON HUTTER*
*who dreamed dreams*
*and believed in books*
*as he did his fellow humans.*
*He forgave everything in us*
*but imperfection.*

# Contents

# The Concept of the Zoo

Since its inception, the zoo has known many forms and served many purposes. It has alternately been a symbol of wealth and power, a source of profit, and the object of a developing humane community's wrath. Today, the zoo has become a privilege, not a right, with a responsibility both to reveal the biological heritage of our earth and to maintain it. With the increasing dominion of man over the planet, it is the last port in a terrible storm of destruction. More than offering a lesson in natural history, the zoo and the history of its evolution provide a lesson in growing humanity.

No one knows when the first crude zoological collection was assembled, but it was certainly done without a scientific plan. The sciences involved in such an undertaking didn't even exist at the time.

Live exotic birds, mammals, and reptiles were part of early trade and tribute. Peacocks from Asia, cheetahs from either Asia or Africa, wading birds and parrots are all recorded in pictures and in words as gifts presented to the mighty to gain attention and curry favor. At what point the actual menagerie emerged we will never know because we can't determine where it happened first—China, perhaps, Egypt, or some ancient nation-state in Africa, Asia, or the Middle East that no longer exists in any recognizable form today. It is logical that at some point someone of importance kept the oddities and curiosities of exotic lands out of interest in the animals themselves. Perhaps the first menagerie was a gift to a child, to an heir to a throne, to a queen or perhaps a favored concubine. It was assembled, probably at enormous cost, to amuse someone.

There is the essence of it: it was done to amuse. The animals may have been kept for a short time and then eaten as an act of ostentation or in a ceremony. Perhaps they were released within an enclosed area and hunted. That kind of "hunting" was popular in medieval times and surprisingly continues into our own; in fact, it has become big business in Texas and elsewhere.

There was probably a competitive edge to maintaining exotic animals. Perhaps having the most exotic animals or the strangest was a mark of accomplishment. The animals could have been symbols of how far the mighty lord's influence was felt. They indicated, certainly, from how far tribute came.

It is reasonable to assume that some animals kept in ancient menageries reproduced. That would be virtually inevitable with a good many species; but a concerted program for husbandry was unlikely to have been part of any early plan. It is also unlikely that nutrition was a major concern as long as the animals lasted for a while and were replaceable. Cages must have been small, if we are to go by what came even millennia later, and the animals probably suffered. It is likely that no menagerie of any size could have existed outside of a warm climate; tropical forms, the most likely to have been collected, would never have survived.

We know that exotic animals for display and for gladiatorial games were maintained in Rome and in outlying Roman possessions. We know that medieval princes hunted with cheetahs and falcons and that even exotic domestic animals, dog breeds especially, were part of the trade caravan's cargo. There was so much traffic back and forth involving some domestic breeds—poodles and mastiffs, for example—that we don't know where the breeds evolved by selective breeding. There are a great many theories and few facts.

The zoo in Vienna has been on its present site since the 1700s, so we know the idea entered modern times as an established institution. But even in the 1700s the zoo was really a menagerie.

There is no finite separation between the words *menagerie* and *zoo* except that the first is an older concept and the latter, which is short for "zoological garden" or "zoological collection," is more modern. The earlier word carries a bad connotation today, whereas the word *zoo* need not. As recently as a decade ago, zookeepers in New York City (in the then city zoos—*not* at the private New York Zoological Society's world-class facility in the Bronx, the Bronx Zoo) were listed on the civil service budget sheet as *menagerie keepers*. There was no such thing, according to New York City's budget office, as a zoo director. In the world's supposedly most progressive city that person, the zoo boss, was listed simply as a *senior menagerie keeper*. The keepers were on a lower salary base than city employees categorized as *labor-*

*ers.* This is menagerie thinking of classic hue. And there was more than semantics involved. The city zoos were appallingly bad, with small cages, no staff veterinarian, and far too many animals, frequently of the wrong kinds. Fortunately, that is history. The New York Zoological Society has taken over the city's zoos, to the relief of everyone.

Zoos all over the world have taken the brunt of the rage of the humane community for somewhat over a century since the imperative for the humane treatment of animals was formalized into societies with specific goals. The Royal Society for the Prevention of Cruelty to Animals was established in England and, in the middle of the nineteenth century, brought to New York City by Henry Bergh and to Boston by George Angell. Initially horses, among the most mistreated of all animals, were the main targets (along with mistreated children), but interest in conditions in zoos came along in time. Slowly the humane zoo that was built on scientific principles evolved.

There are four pillars upon which the modern zoological collection stands. Amusement, probably the motive for the first collections several thousand years ago, is one, now somewhat updated to be called recreation. That use of wild animals is no longer limited to princes and nobility. Most zoos are set in or near urban environments and provide a rare opportunity for city dwellers to see first hand the magnificent forms of wildlife with which we are supposed to coinhabit our planet. Many zoos, like the famed facility at San Diego, as well as Cincinnati, and Sedgewick County in Wichita, Kansas, are both zoos and botanical gardens combined. The main entrance to the Bronx Zoo is directly across the street from the New York Botanical Garden, offering visitors their choice of experiences with living forms.

The second pillar of the modern zoo is education, and in a fine zoo the two goals of recreation and education are so skillfully blended that the visitor is not aware where one stops and the other takes over. Excellent zoo graphics help achieve the blend. Fine interpretive displays play a major role. The insect house at the great Cincinnati Zoo is an example. Visitors pass through a veritable maze of graphic displays and living specimens, both learning and enjoying at the same time. Simple, everyday devices are adapted and made part of the experience. Children are invited to step onto a scale that measures them not in pounds but in numbers of insects. It is a lesson in perspective.

At the Cincinnati Zoo, something of a hallmark institution, there is even a high school; part of the regular city school system, where youngsters with zoological aspirations gain their education. It is a kind of ultimate involvement by a zoo in education.

The third pillar is research. The concept of research with living animals is another flash card that earns the ire of many in the humane community. In the zoo, though, vivisection (literally, "cutting into living animals") is not what is meant. Reproductive physiology, parasitology, and nutritional studies provide the products to be fed back out to wildlife biologists and managers for the good of the species in the wild and need not intrude on the comfort or safety of captive animals. Much has been learned by observing behavior, too. It is obviously true that lions and tigers, elephants and small whales are too far removed from anything like a natural setting to provide very many meaningful clues to natural behavior (after all, predators can't hunt and prey animals can't avoid their enemies) but smaller animals kept in natural settings are useful. Research in zoos is a very broad field and it is properly reserved for another volume to define and explore.

The fourth pillar of the modern zoo is captive propagation, and that is the part most often referred to in this book. As we shall see, case by case, many species of animals now survive only because of zoos and in increasing numbers more, unfortunately, must be added to that list every year. If they are not, they will vanish. The zoo is not the whole answer to wildlife's needs, but it is now an important part of the equation for more and more species.

All of the modern techniques used with livestock—artificial insemination, matching breeding stock with computer guidance, embryo transfer where the inseminated egg of a rare animal is transferred painlessly to the body of a common but related species to free the rare animal to produce more eggs more often—have become commonplace. Sperm and even zygotes or fertilized eggs can be stored in liquid nitrogen for later use. All of this has been done with domestic livestock except, perhaps, the wondrous concept of moving embryos from species to species. Horses now carry zebra fetuses to term. The eland, a relatively common giant antelope, has successfully given birth to the far rarer bongo. Neither mother nor child seems to know or care about their inherent differences. The surrogate mothers, of course, simply provide a biological envelope for the fetus and have no genetic input at all. Things have come a long way from the almost certainly cruel status symbol of the ancient menagerie. ISIS (the International Species Inventory System) is a kind of computer-controlled lonely hearts club for zoo animals as well as an inventory. Member zoos have the genetic histories of all their animals on file so appropriate matches can be made. Studbooks variously kept in zoos around the world are species-by-species records to the same end.

The SSP referred to in our text is the Species Survival Plan, an in-zoo and inter-zoo project again as species-by-species programs. The Redbook referred to in the text is the listing published in multiple volumes by the International Union for the Conservation of Nature headquartered in Switzerland. The worst status an animal can have is "endangered," which means that the animal is in actual danger of extermination. The next in line is "threatened." Those animals listed as threatened are also seriously in harm's way. When we refer to a species as "protected," we refer to actual acts and laws that have been enacted to help it survive. Laws concerning animals both wild and domestic mean a great deal more in some societies than others.

Although it is not practical to place every animal in a setting perfectly natural to it, enormous strides have been made in providing *naturalistic* settings. We may assume animals are more content wandering across large open areas than they are in metal and concrete boxes. It can be a very difficult problem keeping vegetation intact when animals such as great apes and elephants are involved, because they will destroy anything that grows just to entertain themselves. Security is also an ongoing problem although escaping animals are the least of it. Animals seldom escape. People, however, are not always responsible in their own actions, and visitors have to be kept from joining the animals in their display enclosures. There is, too, the problem of deranged visitors providing food or throwing other objects that can be deadly. Zoo animals have regularly been killed by people of both good and evil intent. Still, these problems are all predictable and modern zoos have taken enormous strides to anticipate and prevent accidents to visitors and animals alike. The natural-like setting is the way of the modern zoo in as many cases as possible. The problems with nocturnal animals that would never be seen by the visitor or largely subterranean species have to be accommodated in special displays, virtually always indoors. There is, too, the problem of climate. Warm-weather species such as the apes can't be out in higher latitudes during the winter months. It is generally more expensive to display animals in colder climates. The only way to offset that problem is by judicious species selection. Not all species, obviously, belong in every zoo. In fact,

the zoos that truly limit their collections to the animals they can display best are almost always the best zoos. Only huge institutions like the New York Zoological Society, San Diego, and the Cincinnati Zoo can afford to come close to all-weather, any-species collections.

In no sense is this book an apology for zoos. Poor zoos exist and if they can't be upgraded to modern humane and scientific standards, they should be closed down or at least their collections should be thought through with great care. There is never an excuse for an inhumane zoo and, although not every zoo in every community can really do much in the way of research or perhaps add very much by rare-species propagation, zoos can provide experiences in natural history and education in conservation. They can provide an education in humanity. Those that cannot do at least that much by being humane to the animals in their care should be phased out. A community that does not keep a fine zoo, however small it is, has no reason to have a zoo at all.

There are people of perfectly good intent who feel that all zoos should go and that we have no right to keep animals captive for our amusement. In our opinion that is a short-term view. The fourth pillar of the zoo, captive propagation, in our opinion, not only justifies fine zoos, it mandates them. It is an argument that goes around and around endlessly, and we cannot resolve it here except to offer our own somewhat educated views.

There is not very much mystery about where the zoo of the future must head. It simply must get better and better, being always more humane and always mindful of its place in science, education, and the life-style and values of the people who come to see and learn while being entertained. Fine-tuned projects such as interspeices embryo transfer and nutritional studies seldom involve the visitors, although the former always provides excellent copy for local newspapers and radio and television stations, and it brings in the crowds upon which the zoo very much depends. A zoo is like a theater. It can't play to an empty house for long and to avoid that, the show has to be good.

The zoo should, like any fine public spectacle, appear effortless and self-perpetuating. It can never be either, but that is not for the public to worry about. Zoos, for the general public, are places to enjoy, places where they go to seek beauty and wonder and to sample, rather close up, the most exotic living experiences our planet can offer.

Zoos offer incredible opportunities to photographers and indeed a good many displays are designed with the popularity of photography as a hobby in mind. The next time you visit a zoo, note how many people have both home video and still cameras with them. Some are taking snapshots, of course, kids in front of the elephant display, while others are doing serious portraiture.

Wildlife photography *in the wild*, is an art and a science, but it is something relatively few people get to do very much of. Zoos, however, are at hand and anyone from the novice to the ultimate professional can find incredible opportunities for fine portrait studies. As time passes the zoo is becoming just about the only place anyone will ever get to photograph a lengthening list of species. This book pays tribute to the patience, determination, and skill of many photographers whose names appear in an appendix to this book. They have taken the zoo as an outstanding photo opportunity and have recorded for themselves and for our children some of the animals that have been "taken in from the cold." They have made it possible for this book to be a record in word and picture of some of the zoo's better known or more interesting animals, a representative one hundred, most of which we would lose were it not for the work zoos are doing. The results of all that patience and skill are photographs that are often works of art but with scientific validity and value. They provide a gallery that is aesthetically pleasing (an ultimate form of recreation) and should be, at the very least, educational. They are perfectly in keeping with the mission of the zoo itself.

A word on how the pictures and therefore the species in this book were selected. This book is a sampler, a whip-around the zoo to see what is going on there and where the future appears to lie. The purpose of the book is just that, a look at the present and an educated guess as to the future. The list and indeed the order in which the animals appear could be done over again in hundreds of combinations, but there is no one way to visit the zoo. However, through the efforts of photographers both amateur and professional we have compressed many of the world's best zoos into one outing. The only ordering of the animals is a breakdown into three broad geographical divisions: Africa, Europe/Asia/Austro-Pacific, and Western Hemisphere. Enjoy your zoo visit.

AFRICA

# Leopard

## PANTHERA PARDUS

The leopard *(Panthera pardus)* should not be confused with the clouded leopard or the snow leopard. They are distinctly different species. It is one of the most adaptable carnivores in existence. Its range is enormous, from Turkey to Siberia, from the Arabian Peninsula to Israel, to the Malay Peninsula, Java, Sri Lanka, India, Bangladesh, any number of other Asian states, and most of Africa. It is able to range anywhere there is food and cover. It inhabits dense steaming jungles, mountain as well as lowland forests, semiarid regions, deserts, open flatlands and savannas, high rocky areas where snow is present for a good part of the year, and in fact, almost anywhere, including the outskirts of large cities like Nairobi. It is a tough, elastic animal.

When the all-consuming fur trade was still able to market spotted cats with impunity, the leopard population was reduced in some areas; but now that leopard skin is not much used, and it is illegal to take the cats and attempt to export them, those populations are coming back. It has been on the "big five" list for hunters in Africa—along with lion, elephant, rhinoceros, and Cape buffalo—for generations. Enormous numbers were taken as trophy animals. The same is true in Asia.

The leopard belongs to one species over its enormous range. Its appearance does vary, however. The ground color behind its spots and rosettes varies from pale straw to gray buff, fulvous, ocher, and chestnut to black. The black, or melanistic, phase is far more commonly reported in Asia than Africa, in forests rather than open country. Black leopards can crop up almost anywhere within the species' range, however, and it is always startling when they appear. The black phase is generally referred to as the black *panther*, but the species is the same. Black and spotted leopards can appear in the same litter. Black cats can have spotted young and vice versa. In fact, the black leopard or panther has spots and rosettes that can be easily detected in slanting rays of sunlight. On the subject of spots: cheetahs have spots, or in *extremely* rare cases stripes; jaguars have spots within rosettes; and leopards have rosettes on their body with spots on their head, forequarters, and legs.

A studbook for captive leopards is kept at the Riverbanks Zoo in Columbia, South Carolina, and there are rare subspecies with relatively few captive specimens recorded, such as the Sind leopard, Nepal leopard, Ceylon leopard, Korean leopard, South Arabian leopard, and Indo-Chinese leopard, to name a few. But in total, hundreds of leopards are now being held in zoos all over the world. Many zoos specialize in one subspecies or geographical race, while others are not always certain of the origin of the line they are holding. Although all are members of a single species, every effort is made to keep known races and subspecies apart and distinct. Records are essential; without them, it is not possible to be certain about a leopard's origin.

It will never be possible, as far as we know now, to return leopards to the wild. They learn to hunt from their mothers, and a hungry leopard without that education is certain to get into serious trouble. If it doesn't starve, it will attempt to take livestock or even human beings. There are animals such as porcupines and constricting snakes, and a leopard could die attempting to take them for a meal. The world is a dangerous place for a relatively small cat that is under two hundred pounds, even for a large male. Only the clever and well indoctrinated are likely to survive in it. Bigger cats seen in captivity have become obese from a far too easy life.

Loss of habitat automatically means loss of natural prey, which in turn forces the leopard up against the interests and well-being of man, who will eliminate leopards from a number of areas where they now survive. That will mean the extinction of some subspecies, which may or may not be represented in zoos. Not unlike the coyote in North America, however, the leopard will undoubtedly survive well into the next century, and perhaps even the next. It is resourceful and resilient in or out of the zoological collection.

2

# Cheetah

## ACINONYX JUBATUS

The cheetah *(Acinonyx jubatus)* once ranged widely on the Indian subcontinent and in Asia Minor as well as Africa. The African populations are the only ones left today. The animals were so widely hunted in Asia and in the Middle East that they simply crumbled under the assault and vanished. It is believed that an English trophy hunter killed the last known specimen in India in the 1950s.

The fur of the cheetah is poor, but the fur trade demanded its share for hats, muffs, purses, and other fashion accessories. Occasionally a fur coat was made of cheetah skin, but it didn't keep anyone warm.

The cheetah is known for its speed. It is true that in short spurts, for perhaps a quarter of a mile, it can reach seventy miles an hour. Its legs appear to be far more canine than feline in character, and its claws are nonretractable. It is the only cat of which this can be said. It is not a climbing cat although one will occasionally jump up onto a very low branch. It is not an animal of the forest but of the open savanna. The speeds it attains while hunting would be suicidal with the many obstructions it would encounter in the forest.

The prey of the cheetah are the smaller antelopes and other small, fast animals like rabbit and hare. It cannot take larger prey and is often the victim of lion and leopard, whose ranges it shares. It regularly surrenders its catch to the more aggressive cats. Its cubs are known to be killed and eaten. It is a very hardworking cat and does not do as well around human development as the other two cats do. Unless it is out in the open stalking prey, it will starve. And out in the open, it is easy to see. Why it was ever considered a trophy animal is difficult to imagine. In a word, the cheetah is *vulnerable.*

The animal pictured here is a freak, in a sense, or at least a rare color or marking variation. It is popularly referred to as the *king cheetah* and until very recently was considered a myth rather than a reality. Then a few turned up in South Africa, and mythology became zoology, as so often happens. The gene that turns a normal cheetah's spots into stripes and blotches exists. This specimen from the Cincinnati Zoo is proof. It differs in no other way from the normal cheetah—in fact it is a normal cheetah, as far as we know, with a recessive gene come to life. What else that gene could carry is not known; so far, nothing has turned up.

The distribution of the cheetah in Africa is obvious—South of the Sahara, east of the forest, out on the savanna. And even there it remains only in pockets. It is no longer hunted legally. It is of no threat to mankind. No records exist of attacks on humans by wild animals. None of the heavier-bodied livestock like adult cattle could be killed by a cheetah, but it must be supposed that calves and goats have fallen. Still, damage would be minimal. Cheetahs, like other cats, will eat carrion. Animals killed by other cats, Cape hunting dogs, or hyenas, unless totally consumed, would be utilized. As so often happens with scavenging carnivores, pugmarks are enough in most people's eyes to make them guilty.

Cheetahs have been kept in captivity and used in sport since ancient times. They were called *hunting leopards.* For many years there appeared to be a secret breeding formula, and very few were born in captivity. The secret is actually in two parts. The female has a cryptic estrous cycle and can be clocked only by the behavior of male cheetahs near her. The second part is that the female breeds with more than one male—polyandry. It is believed that a physician near Rome was the first private cheetah owner to crack the code. A couple living in Phoenix, Arizona—Frank Gilbert and his wife, the late Amanda Blake—apparently recorded the second instance. Since then, cheetahs have been bred regularly in zoos around the world. There is little doubt that with computers to watch the pedigrees of the cats and to advise on proper matching, the cheetah could be maintained without any problem. Breeding loans make it possible to create the best genetic matches.

The problem will come when it is time, if that time ever does come, to return the cheetah to the wild. The incredible increase in human population all over Africa and the pressures that are now making the cheetah's survival there questionable may never abate. Nomadic pastoralists like the Maasai and Samburu will remain hostile to all predators and seek endless vengeance for even a single animal from their flocks that is lost. Then, too, how will tenth- or twentieth- or fiftieth-generation cats ever learn how to hunt, and avoid being hunted, and survive? Such a scenario is difficult to imagine. Before half of the twenty-first century has passed, it is likely the cheetah will be seen only in captivity.

# Caracal

## FELIS CARACAL

The caracal *(Felis caracal)* is one of the small cats, which weighs between thirty and forty pounds, in a genus that is found on every continent except Australia and Antarctica. The only confusion seems to be over its scientific name. It is also listed as being in a genus of its own, *Caracal*, and elsewhere as belonging to *Felis* but with *Caracal* as a subgenus. That doesn't really matter as much as some people seem to feel it does. What does matter is that this handsome lynxlike cat, sometimes referred to as the caracal lynx, had an original range that was absolutely enormous: almost all of Africa, the Arabian and Sinai Peninsulas, at least northwestern India, and Central Soviet Asia, including Turkmenistan and Uzbekistan.

It is not surprising that its range has been shrinking. Populations in Turkmenistan and Uzbekistan are known to be very small and are apparently confined to fairly isolated pockets such as the Kopet Dagh Mountains and the Kara Kum Desert near the Iranian frontier. They probably do not range down into Iran now, although almost assuredly they once did. There are thought to be at least nine subspecies, seven of which come from Africa. In Africa, they almost cover the continent excepting the rain forest belt of West and Central Africa. They are cats of open country—savannas, plains, semideserts, even rolling sand deserts in lowlands and hills, as well as mountains. They are extremely adaptable and when left in peace are successful at finding an available niche and filling it. They hunt mammals from the smallest rodents to the smaller antelope such as the reedbuck. They eat any birds they can take, being agile enough to catch low-flying birds on the wing. They will even take poisonous snakes, again being agile enough to outmaneuver even a frantically striking reptile that is perfectly capable of killing its tormentor if it misjudges a move. Unfortunately, a caracal will also kill sheep, goats, calves, and domestic poultry if that is what is at hand when the cat is hungry.

The athletic agility of these cats is so remarkable they were kept as trained hunters in Persia and India to hunt hare and birds. Watching them was a favored pastime of the wealthy and powerful. Cheetahs were kept in the same palaces and courts to hunt larger game like antelope; falcons were used on high, fast-flying birds.

Because the caracal is mainly crepuscular (active at dawn and dusk) and nocturnal, it is not often seen by people living or traveling in its territory. Caracals can be active during the day if they are hungry enough. They climb well, use burrows, hollow trees, rock piles and caves, and thick brush. They are the undisputed masters of taking advantage of whatever their surroundings have to offer. They are archsurvivors above all else. They will even eat new grass and some fruit when that is what is handy. They stalk prey or drop on it from overhead, from trees or rocks—whatever works at the moment.

As might be expected of a cat that adapts so well to a wide variety of opportunities and problems in the wild, the caracal does extremely well in captivity. Specimens (frequently breeding pairs) are exhibited in dozens of zoos. Thirty or forty births from captive breeding a year is not an unusual census. Like most of the lesser cats, the caracal pales somewhat as an exhibit when compared with lions, tigers, leopards, snow leopards, and jaguar, but the appearance of cubs is generally welcomed by the faithful zoogoer.

The caracal now being produced in zoos will almost certainly not go back to the wild; nor will their offspring. The two populations, captive and wild, must be considered as forever separate and apart. Fortunately, caracal in the wild are seldom affected by deforestation. Although they may be poisoned, trapped, and hunted when they become too much of a nuisance to farmers and husbandrymen, they will probably be among the last of the cats to go. Still their range is smaller and more discontinuous than it used to be or should be now. If that trend continues as a descending line on a graph, the caracal, too, could feel the pressure of explosively expanding human populations. Care must be taken, for no predator is really safe in the wild.

# Sifaka

PROPITHECUS VERREAUXI

The sifakas, animals indigenous only to Madagascar, have been thought to consist of just two species in their own genus, *Propithecus*. They are strange, lanky pre-monkeys, or prosimians, with very elongated hind legs. They spend most of their time in tall trees and leap up to thirty feet at a time, using their powerful hind legs for propulsion. They are usually spotted thirty to forty feet above the ground. Their diet consists of leaves, flowers, fruit, and bark. On those occasions when they do come to earth after some choice food, they run around on those long legs, waving their forelegs above their heads for balance.

One species, Diadem sifaka *(P. diadema),* from east and north Madagascar, is little known but is listed as endangered, apparently seriously so. It is believed to have four subspecies. Verreaux's sifaka, *P. verreauxi*, is also recognized as having four subspecies and comes more from the west and south of the great island. All of its four subspecies are listed as endangered, too. The sifakas were once protected by a taboo against harming them, but cultures tend to loosen up in time and the taboo as a shield for these animals has just about vanished. The big threat is, of course, forest degradation, or even total destruction. The latter scenario is being played out in ever expanding areas on Madagascar.

The life-style of the sifaka is very monkeylike. Their strange name comes from a barking alarm signal, one of several variations of the sound *sifaka*, which it gives when there is danger below on the ground. Small bands of from four to fourteen sifaka travel a home territory together with a neat family hierarchy in place for nine months of the year. Everything seems to come apart between January and March, during the mating season. As dominance shifts, males leave one group to take over another, and the females hold themselves for males that are proven commanders. Then, after the mating is over, everything falls into place again. The male that was dominant during mating season may slip quietly into second or even third place, and there is peace for the balance of the year. Vocalizations are frequent and varied with the *sifaka*-like call being just one of many.

There are very, very few sifaka of any species or subspecies outside of Madagascar. However, the Duke University Center for the Study of Primate Biology and History has the genus as a project for captive breeding. That bodes well for a breakthrough that could spread expertise and breeding stock to other institutions. There have been *P. verreauxi* at Duke since 1962 in what has been the only captive breeding colony of the species in the world.

In 1987, the same facility established a captive breeding program for *P. diadema*, the more seriously endangered species. That was when the third species of sifaka was defined. In 1988 Dr. Elwyn Simons announced that Tattersall's sifaka, *P. tattersalli*, as a species was valid. Formerly thought to be a subspecies of *P. diadema*, it was discovered to be unique in many ways when specimens were captured for shipment to the Duke Primate Center. Had there not been a plan to put what had been learned with Verreaux's sifaka to work for the Diadem sifaka, the Tattersall species would almost certainly have become extinct, without it ever being recognized that it had once existed. Such is the role a captive breeding program can play, whether it is in a zoo or a facility like Duke. Duke, however, is unique in the world of the lower primates.

The sifakas may very well not survive in the wild on Madagascar. Whether it will be enough to maintain captive breeding colonies of these exceedingly rare animals is something that may not be known for many years. It is certain, though, that as long as it is possible to keep the species and subspecies, alive, it must be done. To allow these rare and important animals simply to vanish is unthinkable.

# Ring-Tailed Lemur

## LEMUR CATTA

The great land mass of Madagascar broke free from the mainland of Africa somewhere on the order of one hundred million years ago. The vast island is nearly a thousand miles long—the distance, roughly, from Boston to Atlanta. In its splendid isolation it has developed its own fauna and flora, 90 percent of which is endemic, found nowhere else in the world.

Between fifteen hundred and two thousand years ago, the first Malagasy arrived from Indonesia in outrigger canoes, an astounding journey. And the plants and animals of this unique region were apparently doomed. There are now twenty tribes on the island, which they think of as a continent. They all speak one language even if they live by the standards and traditions of distinctly different cultures. In total, man has cleared about 80 percent of the land in many areas, actually destroying the soil in the process or at least as the outcome of attempts at intensive agriculture. As a result, the incredible animal life that evolved after the island's separation from Africa is in trouble, potentially all of it.

Best known, perhaps, are the lemurs. There are seven species of dwarf and mouse lemurs, sixteen of the large lemurs, four species of leaping lemurs, and that one strange species called the aye-aye with which we are also concerned in this book. Depending upon which authority you accept, there are somewhere between twenty and forty species of lemurs, none of which are found anywhere on this planet but Madagascar, with the exception of a very few species found in limited numbers in the Comoro Islands at the northern end of the Mozambique Channel between Madagascar and Africa.

The lemurs are well up from the bottom of the primate family tree, but still below the most primitive monkeys. They evolved on the great island over an extraordinary period of time and now face the prospect of extinction in the wild.

The genus *Lemur* contains six species of what are generally referred to as the large lemurs. (Lemurs once existed that were the size of chimpanzees, but they have long since become extinct. They apparently did coexist on the island with man.) In this group is found the very handsome ring-tailed lemur *(L. catta)* from the southern part of the island. It is inquisitive, gregarious, peaceful, and has the enchanting habit of sunning itself by walking around on its hind legs with its forelegs or "arms" spread wide appearing for all the world like other worldly sun worshippers.

The ring-tailed, like all of the other species, could be crushed out of existence by habitat destruction. Although 80 percent of the island has already been cleared, deforestation is continuing as it always has since man claimed the whole land mass for himself to the exclusion of all other species. Fortunately, this quiet, sensible species does very well in captivity. Two hundred or more are born in zoos and private collections every year.

It is unlikely, therefore, that the ring-tailed lemur will actually become extinct since there are breeding colonies already in place all around the world. Neither natural catastrophe nor an outbreak of disease is likely to do the captive animals in no matter what happens on the island of Madagascar. But if the destruction of the remaining lemur habitat on the island were to continue, where could the animals ever be restored? We would have, in chosen locations on six of the seven continents, living and reproducing museum specimens. It is not a matter of political instability that can and usually does pass in a relative short historical span. The very island itself is being changed, perhaps irreversibly, and that process is already almost two millennia old.

There is no question that the zoos must continue in their breeding programs and disperse ring-tailed lemurs into ever more collections. Fortunately, they are interesting, attractive animals for zoo display. But where is it all to end? How many species—animals the rest of the world has apparently abandoned—can the zoos of the world, even the best and the richest of them, continue to accept total responsibility for?

# Giraffe

## GIRAFFA CAMELOPARDALIS

There were once a large number of species on this planet that we would place in the family Giraffidae. They ranged widely over Africa, Asia, and Europe. There was even an antlered giraffe in Africa. They are all gone now except for two species, the okapi of forested country in western Africa and the giraffe of open plains and savannas to the east. There is only one species of giraffe left *(Giraffa camelopardalis)*, although it does have races and subspecies: the distinctive reticulated giraffe has a more northerly range than the Maasai giraffe, there is a subspecies known as the Angola, one called the kordofan, and a Uganda or Baringo (a.k.a. Rothschild). They all do, however, belong to that single species.

Giraffes are the tallest animals on earth. The presumed record for a bull is about twenty feet, actually one inch under that. The greatest recorded weight is believed to have been 3,969 pounds, only thirty-one pounds short of two tons. It is interesting to note that despite their enormously long necks, giraffe have the same number of cervical vertebrae—seven—as man or any other mammal. But they are very large neck bones.

All giraffes today are found in fairly open country south of Sahara, but as recently as fourteen hundred years ago, they ranged north of the desert. They graze on the tops of trees, well above the browsing range of any other animal except a busy elephant with a long trunk. Elephants can knock trees over when they want vegetation or fruit that is high up, something giraffes don't do.

The different forms of modern giraffe have two, four, or sometimes five knobs or "horns" that can be devastating when swung in a sweeping arc by that tremendously long and powerful neck. Bulls do engage in a certain amount of combat, using the necks and knobs. Giraffes also kick with the forefeet. A three-thousand-pound animal can deliver a very serious blow with a very long leg.

Giraffes adapt surprisingly well to human intrusion. They are common animals on farms and ranches and even along heavily traveled highways. They are peaceful, sensible, intelligent, and very curious. Tourists on horseback can insinuate themselves into a group of giraffes with perfect safety and without causing alarm among the animals. It is best, however, to use horses that are used to seeing and smelling giraffes. An uninitiated horse coming upon an animal taller than the trees might very well try to climb a tree at first sight.

Giraffes flourish in zoos. They should have a well-thought-out enclosure. Usually exhibited behind moats today, they need plenty of food placed high up and a ready supply of water. They are spectacular animals to see although it must be noted that they are even more spectacular in the wild, where they can be seen often and in large numbers. As many as 150 giraffes are likely to be born to the world's zoos in any given year. Some years, the count is even higher. They serve a double value because they are so spectacular in the zoo and because they constitute a reserve that could supply animals for the wild if it ever becomes necessary.

The problem with the giraffe is that it is so accepting of human activity and fits in very well where livestock is kept, since it does not compete with them for browse. If the wild areas in giraffe country ever need restocking, it will probably be because the area has been so seriously impacted by man that giraffes, either wild-born or captive bred, simply can't survive there at all. In that sense the giraffe is a kind of barometer of how things are going.

As for relatively rare races and subspecies, the zoos will have to define them and breed them with careful attention to pedigree. They can all interbreed but there is little point in producing hybrids when pure-bred animals are as easily come by. The most spectacular of all giraffe forms is the reticulated giraffe, and they are in good supply in zoos as well as in Kenya.

Giraffes have been seriously reduced in numbers in modern times by overhunting for trophies and for their meat, which is very tough but tasty, and for their sinews and hides. Some forms, like the Egyptian, were killed off between two and three thousand years ago. They were gone from Morocco by A.D. 600. In this century, they disappeared from most of southern Africa. Because of their quiet tolerance of man, we must assume those that have gone disappeared because of direct destruction. Hopefully that activity is now dying down, and the giraffe will be able to hang on.

# Suricate

## SURICATA SURICATTA

The suricate, or slender-tailed meerkat *(Suricata suricatta)*, is the only species in its genus and should not be confused with the gray meerkat (a.k.a. Selous's mongoose—*Paracynictis selousi*). The suricate, a member of the mongoose family Viverridae, is not a weasel although often thought of as such by the uninitiated. The weasels, family Mustelidae, are different animals although both families are in the order Carnivora along with dogs, cats, bears, raccoons, and pandas.

The range of the suricate is across a good part of southern Africa, South Africa proper, Angola, Namibia, and Botswana. These little four-foot-long animals (that includes a nine- to ten-inch tail) may weigh as much as two pounds. The females are 20 percent larger and heavier than the males.

The suricate is a creature of dry, open land and is an efficient burrower. It may share a burrow with ground squirrels and live in harmony. If the ground is too rocky for digging, the little family units will den in rocky crevices. They hunt for insects, other invertebrates, eggs, and, it is believed, some vegetable matter. Because their food demands are not exotic or competitive with man, and since they prefer rocky dry ground, which would be poor for agriculture, they are not in conflict with man. Only almost total habitat destruction for activities like industrial development and mining should cause them really significant difficulty.

Suricates (unlike Selous's mongoose) make very good pets, as they are affectionate, playful, and quite engaging. Many households within their range keep them as pets and for control of rats and mice, which they will apparently dispatch in true mongoose fashion even though those small mammals are not their natural prey. The suricate does not do as well if it is moved far from its home turf in latitude or altitude. It is very sensitive to cold.

Suricates are highly social animals, with males, females, and young living together. Two or three family units are often found together, often as many as fifteen individuals. There are generally two to five young in a litter, weaned when they are between seven and nine weeks old. Although they are very small animals, gestation is about two weeks longer than that of the dog, about seventy-seven days. One report had a captive animal in San Diego still alive after twelve and a half years.

The suricate is a popular zoo display, although its skill at burrowing means its habitat has to be completely enclosed underground. When an old seal pool is being replaced, more than one zoo has gotten the idea to fill the old one in with rocky soil and start a suricate colony. With a concrete bowl and good high perimeter walls, it works very well, since the animals are diurnal and like sunning themselves in a variety of relaxed postures. As long as the animals are taken in for the winter, a zoo colony can do quite well, and breeding can be expected.

The suricate is not now in trouble as far as current observations go. It has lost some territory to human activity as have all animals. There is every reason to believe suricates will continue to live their inoffensive ways in the wild since their range is large and it is unlikely that much of it will be preempted at any one time. Still, the zoos have a role to play with this species. This animal is one that few people outside of the southern quarter of Africa would ever be likely to see except in zoos. There people can not only see them but know firsthand of one more example of this planet's incredible biological diversity. Captive-bred animals in good supply also mean an area that had been disrupted could be repopulated.

# Drill

## PAPIO LEUCOPHAEUS

There are two spectacular dog-faced forest baboons from West Africa, the drill and the mandrill. They are sometimes placed in their own genus, *Mandrillus,* and sometimes as a subgenus in with the closely related baboons, *Papio.* With no particular advocacy, we will arbitrarily refer to our subject here, the drill, as *Papio leucophaeus.*

The drill is the second largest monkey in the world, weighing between twenty-two and forty-two pounds, with the mandrill being the largest. Both species feed mainly on the ground, seeking everything from fruits and nuts to small animals. They move around in bands, turning over rocks, rotting wood, anything where food might be available in the dense, moist forests they prefer. Although they climb well, they generally prefer the ground, especially the larger males. At night, however, the whole band is likely to take to the trees.

Like its baboon cousins, the drill can be a ferocious animal if its territory, mates, or young are challenged. It will attack even very large animals, including python and leopard, if a confrontation is forced upon the band. The drill and mandrill are both noisy and will retreat in a great flurry of rage if that course is left open to them.

The drill and the mandrill are both so spectacular and colorful that they have always been highly desirable zoo inhabitants. For some reason, the mandrill has been the species more often seen in captivity. In any one year, there may be around sixty drills in zoos while the number of mandrills born in zoos that same year may exceed that number by as much as 20 percent. In a year when about seventy captive-born mandrills appear, there will be only four or five captive-born drills. Both the drill and the mandrill are species that deserve even more attention than they are now getting because they are forest animals, and all forest animals face almost inevitable problems in the short run and catastrophe in the long.

It is fortunate that primates are interesting zoo animals because they can be expensive to obtain, requiring elaborate indoor-outdoor display areas. They must be protected from cold weather, and their diet is very complex. They are amazing escape artists because of their high intelligence and their manual dexterity. Security must be elaborate with routines developed that the animals can't work around. They don't have too much else to do so they have time to watch their keepers and look for openings. Very large baboons like the drill and mandrill can also be dangerous animals, a factor made worse by their intelligence. All of this adds up to an assault on the zoo's budget. If they were less attractive as exhibits, they would be in great difficulty. They would not have the zoo as a backup should their habitat be degraded even further than it has been.

Many African species in the wild are at least temporarily secure because of their power to attract tourists. The list seldom includes deep forest animals, excepting the gorillas, because the tourist traffic in such generally uncomfortable areas is not significant. Hundreds of thousands of people may watch yellow and olive baboons in East Africa, while only a relative handful of people will ever see drills and mandrills in the wild. That poses a problem because people are too often conservation-minded only about species they know, from books and magazines, from television and film, from their own travels, and from zoos. That is where the educational arm of the zoo plays such an important role. If a zoo can propagate a species and provide an emergency backup population, while at the same time make people familiar with the species, it has done its job. If that seems vague or unlikely, consider what the feedback has meant for whale conservation.

Few people were the least bit interested in whales thirty years ago, but once they became familiar with them in aquariums and on television, the hue and cry went up in unprecedented volume. The outrage of ordinary people has resulted in a highly successful whale protection spirit that just may accomplish its work. The only major population center where it has failed to register is Japan.

The same kind of interest has to be achieved for the primates. It is the zoo that must lead the way, along with the media. Very often the media follow the zoo's lead in generating both interest and concern. Hopefully, more zoos will concentrate greater effort in building widespread captive drill populations in ever more attractive, natural displays. The expertise is there. The budget must be adjusted accordingly.

# Bonobo

## PAN PANISCUS

According to Jane Goodall, the world authority on chimpanzees, the so-called pygmy chimp, or bonobo, is probably not as close to the common chimp as the gorilla is, which puts it rather far off to the side of mainstream chimpanzee evolution. It wasn't even accepted as existing until the late 1920s and has been something of a mystery ever since. In 1954, German scientists presented the theory that the bonobo didn't even belong in the same genus as the common chimp *(Pan)*, although it is still referred to as *Pan paniscus.*

The range of these small apes is perilously restricted. They are found only in the forests of the Congo Republic south of the Congo River. The natives hunt them for meat. That along with other intrusions put the remaining bonobos in a dangerous situation. Their habitat is diminishing, and human activity is cutting their numbers. It is the kind of species that could plummet without any more warning than we already have. It has this in common with the increasingly rare mountain gorilla. Fortunately, unlike the mountain gorilla, the bonobo will live in captivity.

In 1960, when a specimen named Kakowet reached the San Diego Zoo, it was an important zoological event. By the mid-1980s, they were found in at least ten zoos and had been bred in San Diego as well as in zoos in Germany and Belgium.

The bonobo differs from the common chimp in a number of ways. It is less than half its larger cousin's size. It is much milder in disposition and not given to wild tantrums as regular chimps are. Its skull is rounder, its body more slender, and its second and third toes are partially joined. It has smaller ears and reddish lips, which is not so of the larger species.

As its habitat has been intruded upon by man, the bonobo has moved higher into the Ruwenzori mountain massif, out onto the savanna, and has learned how to utilize dry forests and woodlands as well as its preferred rain forests, swamp,

and mountain forests. There is certainly a limit, however, to how far it can be pushed. We may awake some morning and find the species in extreme peril in the wild. This is likely to be true of all of the world's apes eventually.

The bonobo is one of the classic cases where man's ego almost denied its existence. Before it was finally clearly identified in 1928, it was just a rumor. West and Central Africa have been a veritable fountain of rumors for generations—the Congo peacock, the pygmy hippopotamus, the giant sable antelope, and the bonobo all were denied by orthodox science until specimens finally made it essential that they receive recognition. In the meantime, since these species didn't officially exist, no studies were done to give today's wildlife conservationists a base line. We don't know how many bonobos there are, how many there used to be, how far their range spread in prehistoric times, or how many would constitute a healthy wild population today. With so many unknowns, it seems essential that the zoos gird themselves for the worst-case scenario and establish an intense worldwide breeding program based on the best genetic rules and values. The time may not be all that far off before the bonobo will be yet another species for whom captive propagation is the single chance for survival until the world is a safer, kinder place.

One other note: We may suppose that there is no real hierarchy of animals in crisis. One species is as important as another, and all efforts must be put forth to save as many species as possible. However, the true apes—chimpanzees, bonobos, gorillas both mountain and lowland, and the various gibbons—are so extremely close to our line of development that they surely have much to tell us about our origins as well as their own. You can learn something from bones, but nowhere near as much as we really want to know. If there ever is an order of precedence, the apes, including the gentle little bonobo, surely are high on the list.

# Nubian Ibex

## CAPRA IBEX NUBIANA

The splendid little wild goat known as the Nubian ibex *(Capra ibex nubiana)* once ranged from the mountains of Syria, down through the Arabian Peninsula all the way to the Sudan and Eritrea. It is gone from all of that range except for Israel, where it has flourished under total protection since the late 1940s. It has made a signal comeback. Enough young have been produced in semicaptivity to allow unrestricted herds to be established in several areas, including the mountains overlooking the Dead Sea.

The initial captive breeding was done in large open desert compounds near the Red Sea known as Hai-Bar Reserve, the Hebrew word for "wildlife." Bringing back biblical wildlife (of which the Nubian ibex is but one example) was the dream of the late Major General Avraham Yoffe of Israel. He created over two hundred nature reserves as head of Israel's Nature Reserves Authority after retiring from the army to devote his remaining years to conservation. The ibex has become the symbol of the Authority.

The Nubian ibex is a desert mountain animal though it does require a regular supply of water. It is found, then, near oases. The same areas in Israel are also the hunting grounds of wolf, leopard, and hyena, the only animals besides eagles that are able to take the ibex, which weighs up to two hundred pounds and has horns of nearly forty inches. The ibex survives because of its speed and extraordinary agility. It easily negotiates high cliffs and seemingly impossible narrow ledges because of the remarkably flexible structure of its hoofs. It is alert and capable of enormous leaps, straight up or across chasms. It is a difficult animal to catch.

Israel has been able to breed the animals in sufficient numbers to dispatch breeding nuclei to appropriate zoos around the world. The Hai-Bar Reserve is open to the public, and busloads of tourists and schoolchildren arrive daily to see the ibex and other biblical animals. In a sense the Hai-Bar Reserve is a very, very large open-air zoo in a perfectly natural setting. The herds are strong enough now so that even predators are not molested when they turn up. Nature is allowed to sort things out.

The role of misdirected human activity is never far from hand, however, and even the best wildlife conservation stories can have their down sides. The success near the Red Sea prompted the Nature Reserves Authority to establish a second facility in the north near Haifa. Ibex and other animals were moved there to give more people an opportunity to see their national treasures. A raid by Arab commandos was mounted as a harassment technique, and the new Hai-Bar North was set on fire. No one is quite certain exactly how many animals died in the flames, but the death toll was catastrophic. It could be argued that animals should not be required to be players in man's political games.

There is another lesson to be learned in the case study of the Nubian ibex, and that has to do with responsibility. Most zoos whose work and specimens are represented in this book are private. They may receive some financial assistance from cities or states—or from the federal government in the case of the National Zoo, which is part of the Smithsonian Institution—but the backbone of the efforts to save wildlife and educate the public usually comes from members of zoological societies and from fund-raising events. In the case of Israel's Hai-Bar Reserve, there were state and private funds combined, the private funds coming from citizens of Israel and interested parties abroad. The lesson here is that there is no fixed formula. All political units, all citizens of all countries should be (and can be) involved, for the problem is universal, and the results will constitute universal success or failure. Far too often, the people of a country or region look on the wildlife located around them as their property. That is no more true of animals than it is of the air we all breathe.

Each species in need of immediate help or long-term protection represents a different set of political and scientific dynamics. It is far too complex to put to a formula. Whatever works alone or in combination is the solution for that species in that place at that moment. If nothing else, the people who want to see wildlife survive must be pragmatic. The Nubian ibex story is a lesson in conservation pragmatism. Because of a successful captive breeding program, the Nubian ibex, a species that was a large question mark as recently as 1948, is safe, well dispersed around the world, and secure in parts of Israel where political reprisals are highly unlikely if not impossible. You can't be much more pragmatic than that.

20

# Arabian Oryx

ORYX LEUCORYX

In all of Africa and the Middle East, there are only five forms of oryx, of three species. They are antelope midway in size between horses and caribou. They are gregarious and once roamed in large numbers from the Sahara Desert south to arid and grassy areas in southern South Africa. Even in the most arid of the southwestern deserts, the Namib, Mocamedes, and Kalihari, as well as on the flat, hard arid plains of the Arabian Peninsula east of the African continent, this hardy, handsome animal with its huge pointed horns was formerly a common sight, albeit in remote areas.

Since the oryx's habitat is not one highly coveted by man, and still consists of areas with a sparse human presence, it has not been habitat destruction or usurption for agriculture and hydroelectric projects that has driven the population numbers down to the edge of extinction in the wild. In that, it differs from most of the world's other endangered species. The form that concerns us here, the Arabian oryx *(Oryx leucoryx)* has become a rare animal in the wild (if any really exist there at all) because of uncontrolled and mindless hunting pressure.

At one time the Arabian oryx ranged over most of the Arabian Peninsula from Mesopotamia west to the Sinai Peninsula, and north to Syria's desert areas. The ancient Egyptians kept these splendid antelope as captives and hunted them under controlled conditions as well as in the wild. If there are any truly wild herds left at all, they are almost certainly in Oman, but the numbers are assuredly small. After World War II, Arab sheiks, using abandoned machine guns and jeeps along with spotter planes linked to their radio-equipped convoys, chased and decimated the wild herds with the concentrated raking fire of fully automatic weapons. If it wasn't sport, it was apparently a lark! It was one of the more shameful episodes in man's treatment of wildlife in this century, and it was not limited to this one species.

There is now a studbook for the Arabian oryx kept at the San Diego Zoo, and almost certainly all of the hundreds of specimens currently in captivity around the world have been captive-bred. It has been a long time since there were wild Arabian oryx to capture and add to captive stock. Israel has made the species one of its prime objectives in the restoration of animals of the biblical era, and there is a growing herd there at Hai-Bar. Most of that stock came from American zoos.

There is no trouble in maintaining this handsome antelope in captivity. It breeds well, bears healthy young, and forms natural social units. It does require space, however, and a zoo in a tight, limited urban area may have problems maintaining any kind of herd unless it is willing to sacrifice a number of its exhibits for other species. For those zoos with space (or satellite breeding facilities), though, this is a fine target species. As long as breeding nuclei are widely dispersed around the world, disease will not be a problem. As long as the studbook is rigidly followed, genetic stocks should be as diverse and healthy as with any well-cared-for domestic animals. Regrettably, the Arabian oryx is in danger of becoming, like so many other captive animals, semidomesticated. However much effort is put into keeping captive herds wild, they are managed, they do get veterinary care, their nutrition is as carefully managed as if they were expensive racehorses or prize dairy cattle, and they do become accustomed to having people nearby.

Despite the problem of coddling, the Arabian oryx could, in all probability, go back into the wild in a suitable habitat. Original habitat would obviously be best for many reasons, but that will have to be some time in the future when the wild pursuit of oil eases off, when there aren't armies of bored oilfield workers wandering the same country as the oryx, and when some semblance of political stability returns to the troubled lands. At present, the habitat of the Arabian oryx is probably the most troubled area in the world. The oryx just can't face machine guns again, no matter who or what their intended target.

# Klipspringer
## OREOTRAGUS OREOTRAGUS

The splendid little klipspringer *(Oreotragus oreotragus)*, the only species in its genus, comes somewhere between the wildebeest and the dainty oribi on the antelope family tree. It, too, is dainty and diminutive. A tall adult male will stand no more than two feet at the shoulder and weigh about thirty pounds. Only the males generally have horns, although there are exceptions.

The "cliff-springer" is a creature of rocks and lava fields with a style of life not unlike that of the mountain goat. It stands on its tiptoes, on the leading edge of its tiny, almost round hoofs, and hops and leaps from rock to rock in places where there does not appear to be any foothold at all. A klipspringer can land on a projection of rock so small that all four feet are touching, an area no larger than a silver dollar. It browses, mostly, but will eat some grass, working generally in the morning and evening to fill its day's needs. It does drink water, but not regularly, so it can inhabit relatively arid areas. The one requirement it cannot do without, though, is a mass of rocks, where it can rest during the heat of the day and to which it can retreat when threatened. Although shy, it is alert and inquisitive and will stand and stare at newcomers to its territory. Then, suddenly, it is gone. Klipspringers give the distinct impression that they have dissolved into their rocky habitat.

The klipspringer occurs in West Africa, Nigeria, and probably the Central African Republic. It is found in Ethiopia, the Sudan, and from there south to Angola in the west, and South Africa. It may be seen in East Africa as well.

With a range that vast, there is no way to establish population figures, but the species does not appear to be disproportionately distressed. Natives do hunt them for their hides, which they make into utility containers, and for their meat, which is reportedly excellent. At one time, their light and very elastic hair was used to stuff saddle bags and other useful objects that required padding.

Probably fewer than a dozen zoos successfully keep klipspringer and only a few, perhaps six to ten a year, are born. That is enough to demonstrate that with attention to detail, captive propagation is possible. Many of the smaller antelopes are notoriously difficult to maintain and breed. The klipspringer does not live in areas with any real agricultural potential and is in no way affected by deforestation. It is of no use to poachers. A limited number are killed for food by people living near klipspringer habitat, but the species appears able to tolerate the attrition, Many more are killed by python, caracal, serval, leopard, and hyena than by man.

What, then, is the significance of zoos' maintaining these small antelope? Virtually everyone knows about animals like lion, tiger, elephant, and the larger hoofed animals like rhinoceros, zebra, and the flashier antelope, but animals like klipspringer, animals as much a part of the total picture as any of the others, are far less well known. They are almost oddities. It is important that the public be aware of and come to appreciate the critical need for biological diversity. And, too, there is the probability that eventually even harmless, noncompeting, and economically insignificant animals like the klipspringer may be impacted, if not directly by man, perhaps by climatic changes brought about by man. It is also possible that when man has driven away or destroyed other game animals, preempted their land, food, and water for livestock and agriculture, the versatile predators will be driven to rely more heavily on klipspringer than they do now. That kind of pressure could be fatal to any species.

As important as the zoos' role may be in propagating endangered species, they also have an obligation to let people who cannot travel to wild habitats, or are not inclined to do so, see some of the wonderful variations in form and habit that animals have taken in order to grasp a niche and flourish with a minimum of competition. Variability, diversity, is what life and living systems are all about. The zoo is where all of this can be seen when the conditions are right and the zoo lives up to its mandate.

# Eland

## TAUROTRAGUS ORYX

The eland is to the antelope what the moose is to the deer, the largest species in the group. We have to say "group" because the family is Bovidae, which includes the bison, cattle, and buffalo as well. These massive antelope—a really big male can weigh up to a ton or more—carry impressive spiraling horns and are very fast on their feet. One of the most difficult of antelopes to observe or photograph, they are characteristically shy and move away when human beings approach. They are suspicious of everything until they have satisfied themselves that there is no threat.

There are two species sometimes placed in the genus *Tragelaphus*, but as often in *Taurotragus*. The specimen shown here is *T. oryx*, the common eland of the open country from Ethiopia all the way to South Africa. The other species is *T. derbianus*, the Derby or giant eland of the savanna country from Senegal to parts of the southern Sudan. The giant eland is more rich, fawn colored with less of a grayish cast. It also has a black neck with a white band. Record horns of the giant eland measure almost forty-eight inches—an incredible length—and are massive in bulk. Even with their oxlike weight and huge horns, eland are taken by lion. That would explain their shyness when anything approaches them across the savanna.

There have been experiments in domestication, or at least commercially motivated captive propagation in Africa and the Soviet Union. The meat of the eland is delicious; its milk is three times as rich in fat and twice as rich in proteins as dairy-cattle milk, and the hide makes excellent leather. Despite their shyness in the wild, eland settle down extremely well in captivity and are quiet, sensible animals. They live in herds of varying size as wild animals so are easily managed that way on a farm. If man is going to domesticate any more animals, the eland is a likely candidate. It is difficult to say what would come of selective breeding and what a farm eland might look like even after only fifty or a hundred generations. The cows would have larger udders, certainly, and perhaps the horns would be bred out.

Clearly there is no shortage of eland in captivity. The zoos hold many hundreds of the smaller or common eland, although very few of the giant species. The number of common eland bred in captivity each year comes to hundreds in zoos and an unknown number in experimental husbandry facilities. The emphasis in the experiments appears to be largely with the common species but once it has been domesticated and genetic manipulation has begun, the size can be almost anything the husbandrymen want it to be. Since the eland are in the same family with cattle, there is no reason to believe they will be any less flexible.

Because of their size and massive horns, the eland have been irresistible trophy animals and have been targeted by trophy hunters since the earliest recorded safaris. Native peoples, too, have taken them for the enormous amount of meat even one animal can provide. As a result, some races have been seriously impacted, and a western subspecies of the giant form is close to extinction. Fortunately, with at least the common eland, there are enough in captivity to replenish areas that have been secured, which we can hope will eventually occur in some parts of Africa. Unlike predators, grazing animals are easy to reestablish in their original habitat.

The ancestral forms of our domestic cattle, horses, sheep, and goats are either extinct or very close to it. If we are to eventually domesticate the eland, and to an even greater extent than now, its kin the water buffalo, we must make every effort to retain enough unmanipulated specimens of the original animal so that repopulation in the wild will be possible. It is unlikely that commercial interests will assume the responsibility, but zoos already have.

# Patas Monkey

## ERYTHROCEBUS PATAS

The handsome patas monkey *(Erythrocebus patas)* is apparently still to be found in good numbers over much of its natural African range. It is an inhabitant of what is known as the Sudanese Zone, which stretches across Africa at its widest point, from the Atlantic coast in the west almost all the way to the Indian Ocean in the east.

The patas monkey prefers high grassy plains, savannas, and riverbanks, the less heavily overgrown the better. It will often remain near the edge of a forested area on the plains, using the trees for sleeping and the water that is usually found in such oases for drinking. It will move around on rocky plateaus and sometimes even onto cleared fields near human settlements. Patas monkeys are constantly hunting for seeds, fruit, leaves, roots, ground nuts (a cultivated crop), insects, small lizards, and birds. They will also eat any eggs they can get and seek out mineral-impregnated earth. They are adaptable and take advantage of whatever they can find. They do not drink very much water, but must have some available. Trees are for sleeping and lookout posts only. Like baboons, they spend most of their time on the ground.

The patas monkey is a highly social animal. Troops typically have an old male in charge, with up to thirty females and their young. Troops frequently come together at watering places, but there is seldom trouble unless maturing males try to edge into an established troop. The older male will drive them away, and small bands of nonmating males are typical as each animal waits for an opportunity to steal some females or take over a troop. It keeps the older, dominant males on the alert. It is a full-time job, guarding against both enemies and wife stealers.

In the wild, cheetah, leopard, hyena, and hunting dogs, where they survive, prey on the patas monkey. Eagles, particularly crowned eagles, are a threat to the young. A full-grown male, typically twice the size of a female, can weigh about thirty pounds and give a good account of itself in a fight. Still, a cheetah striking at sixty to seventy miles an hour or a gang of hyena or, of course, a leopard would be more than a monkey of even this size could fend off.

In any one year, there may be as many as forty to fifty zoos reporting births of this species. If it could not survive in at least a part of its vast range in Africa, it could survive in captivity, to which, obviously, it adapts very well. Patas monkeys are such handsome animals, given to so much open social interaction, and are such reliable breeders, that they have become zoo favorites. Ironically, this is a species where specimens could be spared by the wild stock, but they are not needed. The patas monkey in our zoos is now capable of being a self-sustaining species.

With so many natural enemies and with some conflict with agricultural peoples being inevitable, why has this monkey been able not only to survive but in some areas flourish while other species dwindle? First, although these are handsome animals, there has never really been a significant market for patas monkey fur. That in contrast with the colobus monkey that has been hunted relentlessly, to extinction in some areas, for its coat. Second, the patas is like the dog-faced baboon group of monkeys, largely terrestrial and is not so seriously or immediately impacted by deforestation as are species that really must have trees or die. One of the most profound insults to our planet in our time, that of the cutting down of entire forests, does the patas relatively little harm. But perhaps the factor that rises above all others is the animal's adaptability. It is a *coping* species and like people, who are able to cope as opposed to rigidly regimented people, it can withstand the problems of an ever-changing planet.

We tend to think of animals that cannot cope with change as being ancient, older at least than the good copers. That may or may not be true, but clearly there is an important distinction between those that can adjust and those that cannot. It is fortunate that there are species like the patas which, although they certainly have their limits, are able to get along. It frees up resources and efforts to get to those species that cannot.

The military medical people call it *triage,* treating those patients first who will live or die according to what is done for them immediately. Our relationship with wildlife today must be largely governed by the same realities. Some species are doomed no matter what we do, some are in trouble but have time and can be gotten to when the urgent matters are attended to first, and some are the urgent matters themselves, species on the brink. Fortunately, the patas monkey, although certainly affected by the exploding human population in Africa, can apparently hold its own for at least a while. It will have to be seen to in time. The fact that zoos have done such a fine job with these monkeys so far makes them even more secure, at least for the time being.

# Red-Eared Guenon
### CERCOPITHECUS ERYTHROTIS

The red-eared guenon *(Cercopithecus erythrotis)* is one of approximately twenty-three particularly beautiful monkeys, known collectively as guenons. Guenons are found in Africa, south of the Sahara, ranging in habitat from forest to savanna. This species is limited to Nigeria and Cameroun, where population studies are difficult, at times dangerous, and almost always unreliable. Political contention in the general West Africa region has created endless problems for scientists trying to determine the status of all wildlife in that vast area.

For the moment at least, the red-eared guenon is a species that is going to have to survive in the wild or not at all. The handsome young male pictured here in the Los Angeles Zoo is the only one of its kind in the United States. It is believed that in the whole world, there are no more than three in captivity. If the word *frustration* required a definition, it would be a zoo director with one specimen of any species. Breeding, of course, is impossible within the zoo, and with so few in captivity, breeding loans are extremely difficult to arrange: No one wants to risk sending such a rare animal, one obviously very valuable and exceedingly difficult to replace, around the corner—much less around the world. It is also difficult with primates because, although some are easy to socialize, others are very picky about their companions and may fight, or worse. It does not look very promising for the red-eared guenon in captivity at the moment. It is, for zoos, a damned-if-you-do and damned-if-you-don't situation.

Things are hardly more promising in the wild. Nigeria has a huge human population that has been in a near constant state of turmoil for decades. It is a very advanced sub-Saharan nation, but wildlife is not viewed there with either passion or concern or, in most instances, even with interest. It is unfortunately true that, except in isolated instances such as parts of India where there are temple monkeys revered by Hindus, primates are just one more form of "beef," be they monkey or ape. They are eaten in an endless number of cultures, and when they are not taken as food, they are killed or driven away because they are perceived as crop destroyers or nuisances at best. Mothers seen with young are likely to be shot in order to recover the baby and sell it for the few coins the international animal trade has to offer at that end of the chain. For those monkeys captured, young or adult, handling and knowledge of nutrition is so poor that most specimens never live to see a destination where survival is possible.. It is an extraordinarily cruel traffic, generally illegal, and a violent assault on the world's vanishing wildlife stocks. Were there to be more red-eared guenons in captivity, it is likely that this wicked pipeline would be involved. What it would cost in suffering and lives to add even three more specimens to the world's captive stock is impossible to calculate.

The plight of the red-eared guenon, a highly intelligent, extremely sensitive animal that is rare in captivity and probably vanishing in the wild at an alarming rate is a red banner of extreme hazard for much of the wildlife in Africa, an area where even half a century ago, there were so many wild animals that few people could even imagine a shortage at any time in the future, much less in four or five decades. There are reports of hunters using small animals such as monkeys to sight in their rifles before going after larger, more exciting game. The small animals were killed without reason or profit, although occasionally a skin was taken for the taxidermist to mount up as a kind of joke in the trophy room. Scientists in their zeal killed far more specimens than were necessary for study collections, and as animals like the red-eared guenon diminish, it would be interesting to see how many skins are in cases laced with mothballs in the world's museums. Of some species, we know, there are thousands representing a time when scientists, from our present perspective, were as much vandals as anything else.

Unfortunately, one specimen of anything was once good enough for scores of menageries where animal husbandry and concern for vanishing species were of little matter. The animals for those collections, little better than stamp collections, really—one of each—came through that same international pipeline discussed earlier. Today, though, in a zoo such as the Los Angeles Zoo with a single male and probably not very good prospects for a breeding female, emotions must hang somewhere between anguish and rage.

From the effects of direct persecution, deforestation, and general indifference, the red-eared guenon may be one animal that our descendants may never get to know.

30

# African Elephant

### LOXODONTA AFRICANA

It is the shocking truth that the largest terrestrial animal left on this planet is threatened with extinction in the wild. As recently as ten to twelve years ago, there were thought to be four million elephants *(Loxodonta africana)* on the African continent. And although that figure was well below what the natural population was deemed to be, it did seem a safe enough position for the species. But now we know the truth. There are probably no more than 600,000 elephants left, and possibly even fewer than that. That is simply not enough for the species to survive unless all human depredation stops immediately. And that will not happen because as these peaceful, highly social giants mature, they develop two specialized teeth known as tusks. Those tusks are made of ivory, an international hard currency.

Poachers, very often filtering southward from Somalia, are slaughtering elephants by the thousands, using everything from trucks to helicopters. Their employers, often political and military leaders, then lift the ivory out and ship it to Hong Kong and Tokyo. There it is warehoused by the hundreds of tons. On the world market, ivory is literally as good as gold. There are ivory hoarders, speculators, wholesale and retail dealers, and auction houses. It is a very sophisticated marketplace, and it will, as seems quite certain now, bring the elephant to the edge of extinction.

Habitat destruction and migratory routes that get chopped up by towns and railroads as well as agriculture all play a role in this mounting tragedy, but poaching is the biggest cause for concern.

Elephants generally survive quite well in captivity, often to their full natural lives of sixty to seventy years, but captive breeding of this species is a rare occurrence. Elephants are as highly social as apes and human beings, and in their natural state, they do not live as couples or even as three or four animals, but in large herds. Under any circumstances, they are very slow reproducers. Single births are the norm (though they can produce twins), and the gestation period is twenty-one to twenty-four months. The young stay with their mothers for years. So even if there were a way to get them to breed in captivity with any degree of regularity, it would be an agonizingly slow process.

As for establishing herds outside of their present natural range, the problems appear insurmountable. A single elephant eats between three and four hundred pounds of greens a day and consumes as much as sixty gallons of water. They are extremely difficult to contain because of their enormous size, and they are naturally migratory. They are also terribly destructive to their own habitat because their digestive system is so inefficient. About half of what they eat passes through them unused. Elephants moving into an area with forest will turn it into savanna in a few years. All of this adds up to animals that have to move or denude the world around them, animals that cost a fortune to feed, make tremendous demands on their environment, and are too costly to contain in the herds they apparently have to live in to reproduce in any reasonable numbers.

No one can say for certain what is going to happen with the magnificent African elephant. Zoos will continue to exhibit them, but they cannot hope to replace those that die off with captive-bred animals. And how much longer we can expect the African continent to supply the zoos of the world is not clear. At the moment it is, quite to the contrary, doing a dishearteningly efficient job of supplying a profit column for one of the bloodiest enterprises on earth. It is going to take some tough resolutions and some very determined warfare to stop the Somalis and the other poachers from wiping the slate clean of all the major species in Africa. It is also going to take some real daring to bring the military and political leaders in Africa, who are behind the slaughter, to justice. With increased worldwide attention being brought to bear on the elephant's extinction, efforts to interdict the poaching trade have increased. But at the moment, there is no cause for rejoicing.

# Black Rhinoceros

## DICEROS BICORNIS

The African black rhinoceros *(Diceros bicornis)* is actually something of a misnomer, since it is the same gray color as all the other species of rhinoceros (members of the family Rhinocerotidae in the order Perissodactyla, the odd-toes ungulates), including the African white rhino. A better name would be prehensile-lipped rhino, since the only other African species, the white, has a square upper lip. It is thought that the word *white* was a mispronunciation by the Dutch-speaking Boers of the word *wide* in "wide-lipped rhino," as the so-called white was once known. The name "black" rhino grew out of an effort to distinguish it from the equally gray but otherwise totally different "white."

Four of the five species of rhino are in trouble to some degree, with the black rhinoceros apparently doomed as a viable breeding population in its native Africa. The white rhino discussed later in this book seems relatively safe at the moment. In Asia, especially in the world's two most heavily populated nations, China and India, rhino horn is used as an aphrodisiac as well as a cure for just about every disease and undesirable human condition known. Tests show it does none of the things it is supposed to do. It would be ironic if it did work as an aphrodisiac, which is the last thing either China or India needs. The two horns from a single black rhino are believed to have a street value in India of close to a hundred thousand dollars, and the potential profit as the horns move up the ladder from African savanna to teeming Indian city street means, simply, that the rhino cannot survive.

Until very recently, about 40 percent of the poached horns went to the Arab world to make dagger handles. Such daggers are considered the ultimate symbol of manhood and cost at least $10,000. Whether as dagger handles in the most male-dominated chauvinistic societies on earth or as an improver of fertility in humans where improvement is needed least, the horns of these shy, retiring, and very ancient animals have meant their doom.

Throughout Africa today, the black rhino's numbers are plummeting. There is only one reasonably significant population left, in Zimbabwe, and that nation is believed to be losing at least a rhino a day to poachers.

Most of the poaching, as is the case with ivory from the also severely pressured African elephant, is done by Somalis moving into areas where elephants and rhinoceros remain. The poachers are equipped with automatic Russian assault rifles and two-way radios, and they are often controlled by highly placed political and military figures. They do not hesitate to kill game wardens who try to intefere with them. The effort to save the wild rhino can only be described as all-out war.

Fortunately, black rhinoceros do well in zoos. They are bred in captivity around the world, prolifically so in American zoos. At last count, black rhinos in the Cininnati Zoo alone had produced over twenty young in recent years. Another fortunate aspect of the species is that the rhinos can be readily released as wild animals in suitable habitats. It may ultimately be necessary to remove most all of the rhinos from Africa, at least the black, until some of the governments there stabilize and poaching is eliminated. The rhino may have to "come in from the cold" until the world is a safer, wiser place. In the meantime, careful breeding programs in zoos and private collections can keep the species viable and ready for release when the time comes.

# Zebra Duiker

## CEPHALOPHUS ZEBRA

Most people are not familiar with a small group of forest antelope known as forest duikers (pronounced *diker*). There are approximately fifteen species in the genus *Cephalophus C. zebra*, the zebra duiker, will serve here as an example although no more remarkable than the rest. In fact what is said of this species will hold true pretty much for the others. Some are nocturnal and some are diurnal. Their specific food needs vary but the important elements we are able to discuss run through the entire genus.

Duikers in general are secretive and do not collect in large clans or herds; nor do they feed in the open. You are unlikely to see even one in months of travel in Africa. The habitat they require makes it even more difficult to observe them, and they are excessively shy. Other small but open-land antelopes like the gazelles will watch from a few feet away with apparent indifference as cars and trucks roar by or people pass on foot. Virtually any movement or noise, on the other hand, will send a shy duiker running for ever deeper cover. The animals' small size, their build, gait, even their small backward-pointing horns, facilitate easy movement through dense cover, cover often so dense a human being would be hard put to follow.

The duiker's shy ways are not difficult to understand when the list of their probable predators is compiled. Of the cats, the leopard would probably rank first because it does as well in thick cover as the duikers do. Without doubt the python is a frequent predator and one capable of taking a duiker by surprise on the ground or from an overhanging branch. Some of the larger eagles undoubtedly take their share of any duikers that expose themselves for even a moment. Near the water, crocodile certainly must take their share. For these small antelope, the world is a very hazardous place, and if their forests go, so will they. They could never tolerate having lion, cheetah, hyena, and hunting dog added to their list of everyday enemies. Native peoples take them in traps for use as food.

It is generally believed that all of the duikers, including the zebra duiker, are primitive antelope and retain many of the bovid's early characteristics. They apparently depend on their sense of smell as their first warning system, with hearing second and seeing third. For defense, they use hiding.

Their young are easily concealed and all duikers of any age know to freeze at the first sign of danger, the slightest hint of a strange smell, the first suggestion of an unidentified sound. In the deep cover where they spend most of their time, any animal less alert would soon be dead.

In recent years, a number of species of duiker have been kept in zoos but not in large numbers. The zebra duiker has been seen in four or five collections. The specimen shown here is from the Los Angeles Zoo and shows the general form of the group as a whole with the "humped" hind quarters.

The birth of a duiker in a zoo is still a cause for celebration. At least ten duiker species have been bred in zoos, with both Frankfurt and Los Angeles being successful with the zebra duiker. The numbers born or even maintained in captivity have not been sufficiently large to look upon zoos as we know them as the salvation of these increasingly rare animals. With the decimation of tropical forests all over Africa and all over the world, there will have to be preserves as tightly guarded as Fort Knox, or we will see these primitive bovids vanish. They represent a range of biological diversity that simply cannot be spared. Not only their inherent right to survive is at stake but also their beauty and their unimaginable scientific value. With deforestation one of the major catastrophes of our time, all forest animals are in harm's way. As luck would have it, the shy, harmless forest duikers are high on the list of animals that will go as soon as the trees do. Exposed, they are proverbial sitting ducks. If they are not able to live their secretive lives, they can live no lives at all.

For the sake of the duikers, the apes and monkeys, the birds that prefer life under a canopy, for the butterflies and other invertebrates, some areas of the forested world are going to have to be left intact. Unfortunately, it can't be only a few acres here and there. What will have to be set aside are areas of many thousands of acres with forested pathways leading from one to another. Africa will have duikers in its future only if a network of unexploited forest lands are set aside for no other purpose than for the plants and animals that evolved along with the forests themselves to live in close embrace.

# Okapi

OKAPIA JOHNSTONI

The okapi *(Okapia johnstoni)* is one of two species in the family Giraffidae. Both are found in Africa alone, south of the Sahara, and both are browsers. The giraffe, the other species, is found over a vast area in several subspecies and races. The okapi, however, is one of a kind. No other animal is remotely like it. It has a very limited range: only the forests of Zaire. It wasn't even known to science until 1900 although it was a regular item in the diet of the indigenous pigmys.

A studbook for captive okapi is maintained at the zoo in Antwerp, Belgium, and at any one time, there are likely to be between fifty-five and sixty specimens in zoo collections. It is assumed that all of the okapi presently being held were captive born. In fact the world's captive okapi stock may be working off a rather limited genetic foundation. Inbreeding is generally a poor idea because it leads to a reduced ongoing breeding potential, and infant mortality is very much higher. A broader base is needed with more okapi from the wild. But the question is, can Zaire spare any more of these handsome, but probably rare, animals?

Okapi have suffered from man's political instability and social unrest, from an ever-increasing human population, and from deforestation. The okapi is a forest animal. Natives hunt okapi for meat and for their hide, but outsiders rarely ever see one. If the forest is reduced much further, as is happening all over the world where forests still stand, the okapi and all other forest-dependent animals will simply not be there one day. Future generations will surely look at museum specimens of okapi and at any that live on in zoos and wonder why the people of this century and the next did not care enough to protect them.

There is a great deal of discussion about reforestation, the planting of trees after others have been cut down. Paper companies in the United States and Canada, timber companies in Kenya, and countries such as China, Israel, and Iceland have made heroic efforts to replace millions of acres of trees slashed and burned in less thoughtful times. It is true that these massive plantings will clean the air, make the world more quiet, and help stop both desertification and erosion, but unless there is very careful planning, it won't mean a thing for wildlife. Too often reforestation concentrates on fast-growing trees with either timber potential or good root structure to hold soil in place. Rarely does it address the vital concern of diversity. Monoculture, or single-species, re-

forestation schemes ignore wildlife and their needs for food and cover. Forest animals, like the browsing okapi, evolved to utilize a wide variety of forest foods, and it is that combination that provides the nutrients they require.

A single acre of forest in Zaire or any other tropical location might contain between one and two hundred different species of higher or flowering plants. A monoculture reforested area may have no more than a single species of tree and a small variety of lesser weeds or low bushes, if that. There are many such forests in this world, where an okapi or almost any other form of wildlife would starve. From the point of view of wildlife conservation or restoration, trees in and of themselves are meaningless unless they are the right species and of great enough diversity. A natural tropical forest, even a boreal forest, is a spectacular mix, a bewildering combination of plants in all kinds of relationships to each other and to the animals evolved to utilize what they have to offer. That is never so of monoculture forests. There all the trees, all of a kind, stand in rows like obedient soldiers waiting to get tall enough so they can be cut again and replanted from ever-faster growing stock that the geneticists have developed.

The okapi does not do spectacularly well in zoos yet, although it is a handsome and attention-getting display animal. The few okapi born each year in zoos attract a great deal of attention, but it is not enough, not with the world's natural forests in as precarious a condition as they presently are. The forests of Zaire, all the forests from Central to West Africa, are places where secrets are kept and the most mysterious secret of all is their own future. If they go, there is no reason to believe that any restoration done will be any more oriented to the needs of wildlife than such forests have been in other parts of the world.

It is absolutely imperative that we maintain animal diversity by maintaining plant diversity, diverse habitats where each species can get what it needs as it needs it. Since no one really knows what a successfully reproducing, wild-living okapi needs, and since there is no other animal surviving that is like an okapi at all, it might be a very good idea if we let some of the world's forests stand. Zoos can hold species for a time, but the load will one day be too great. Something of the wild is going to have to be allowed to remain unmolested.

# Barbary Ape

## MACACA SYLVANUS

The Barbary ape *(Macaca sylvanus)* is one of the macaques, a group of nineteen species that are all robust if not necessarily large. They have an enormous range across Asia from Japan to Sri Lanka, all the way out to Java, Borneo, and the Philippines. The only one of the nineteen that is native to Africa, the so-called Barbary ape, is a monkey and not an ape at all.

The Barbary ape is something of a mystery because in prehistoric times, it was very widely distributed in Europe as well as northern Africa. When the British arrived on Gibraltar in 1704, there was a colony of the active, inquisitive monkeys there. It is impossible to know if they were a remnant of a European population since Gibraltar is geographically a southern piece of Spain that has gone to sea, or whether they had been introduced to the rock by seagoing traders sometime in the distant past. The population there now is kept at a small enough size to please but not worry tourists. When it has needed bolstering, the small band of thirty to fifty animals has been reinforced by specimens from Africa. When it has gotten too large, some have been trapped and packed off to zoos.

In the latter half of the 1700s, a substantial number of the animals were turned loose in Germany, where they successfully established themselves. Later it was decided that it hadn't been such a good idea and, after about twenty years of freedom, they were purposefully exterminated. The species probably became extinct in Spain in the 1890s, but since that time, some captive specimens escaped there and have successfully reintroduced themselves. They are very adaptable animals. There is presently a large freewheeling and self-sustaining group in France. Macaques generally have been shuffled all over the world, with introductions in Florida, on Mauritius in the Indian Ocean, on Puerto Rico, and on islands off Brazil. Man apparently has just about always meddled with macaques.

What is important about the Barbary ape, however, is its status in its natural range of northern Africa. It is extinct in Libya and Tunisia, part of its former range. In Algeria, it is found only in the mountains between Algiers and Constantine. In Morocco, it keeps to high cedar and oak forests in the Atlas and nearby ranges, to which it is being pushed out by commercial logging. On the plains, it is considered a first-class nuisance animal for the harm it does to crops. At most, there are perhaps 22,000 animals left with more than three quarters of them in Morocco.

As might be expected of an animal adaptable enough to tolerate introduction into China, Puerto Rico, France, Germany, and Spain, it does extremely well in zoos. There are between eight hundred and a thousand in captivity now, and just about all of them are presumed to have been captive bred. Some zoos report a birth or two a year and others fifty, sixty, or even seventy. Clearly zoos can produce as many Barbary apes as they can humanely display. Too many animals, even on a large "monkey island" behind a moat, do not make an attractive display and it isn't good for the animals. They need room to move about and establish normal social groups. Dominant animals must not be too closely crowded in with younger or lesser animals or the results are out-and-out cruel. As with lions, tigers, leopards, and a number of bears, breeding has to be controlled and limited to animals that can be properly exhibited or traded to other zoos for other species. There is no shortage of these monkeys and, like lion and tiger cubs, they are a drug on the zoo market, whatever their status in the wild.

Since there is no problem in introducing Barbary apes, or most of the macaques (family Cercopithecidae) for that matter, into the wild in a great many habitats, it will be possible to return good breeding nuclei to North Africa when preserves are established that can be considered safe. There is no point in returning them when the chances for survival are fair to poor. It is better to hold the reserves in captive colonies than introduce them to areas totally foreign to them where they can do terrible damage to local fauna and flora. Turning animals loose on foreign soil is not the way to preserve species in most cases. Certainly that is the case when they reproduce and spread out like Barbary apes.

# Aye-Aye

## DAUBENTONIA MADAGASCARIENSIS

The exceedingly rare aye-aye *(Daubentonia madagascariensis)* is another one of those animals that is alone not only in its genus but also in its family, Daubentoniidae. It is a surviving twig on what has been an exceedingly complex tree of primate life almost from the start. This rare and seriously endangered species once inhabited coastal areas in both eastern and northwestern Madagascar. Madagascar, the fourth largest island in the world, is second only to Australia in exclusive or endemic species and, unfortunately, endangered species.

As recently as a thousand years ago, there apparently was another species in this family, a much larger animal, *D. robusta*, but it has been extinct since the time of the Crusades. It too was limited in distribution to the one giant island. The cause of its disappearance is not really known, but it is assumed to have been caused by the activities of man. In historical times, there has been practically no other cause recorded. Somewhere in the story of each extinction or endangerment, the heavy hand of man always seems to appear.

The aye-aye eats fruit, bamboo shoots, birds eggs, and insects. It requires tall stands of trees for its strictly nocturnal foraging. The animal is noted for the peculiar third and fourth fingers on each of its forepaws. These digits are extremely elongated, especially the third, and are used for grooming and scratching. It is a peculiar and apparently unique adaptation. They have an unusual feeding behavior. With their long, thin third finger, they tap rotting wood and can tell from the sound if there is a beetle grub inside. If they detect one, they rip away the wood with their teeth and use their long finger with its exceptionally long nail to hook the grub out.

The aye-aye, a relatively shy animal about the size of a large squirrel, simply cannot withstand the ongoing deforestation on Madagascar. It is being driven relentlessly into ever more isolated pockets, and once so trapped and unable to move between pockets where survival might be possible, it is prey to many forces. Further reduction in the number of trees means increased exposure to predation and loss of food. If severely stressed, aye-ayes stop breeding. If they do breed, the strain on them probably keeps them from raising their young. It is believed that reproduction may occur only every second or third year with a single young produced. They are not at all precocious, and there are records of one- and even two-year-old animals still with their mothers. But they are long-lived. The San Diego Zoo had one survive for over twenty-three years. In the wild, however, there is far too much of a strain on animals being constantly crowded and intruded upon.

They were once even thought to be extinct. There are very few aye-ayes in captivity today and records are sparse. We may learn more about the aye-aye in the years immediately ahead than we have ever known in the past, due to the superb Duke University Center for the Study of Primate Biology and History. There the lower primates live in colonies, where they are maintained under ideal conditions and where the reproduction record is one of the best in the world. They have aye-ayes along with many other excessively rare prosimian animals further down the primate tree than monkeys.

On Madagascar, the aye-aye's distinctive bowl-shaped nests occasionally appear in groves of mango trees, planted by the early European settlers, because wild groves of tall trees are too scarce or too far apart. Aye-ayes typically use a nest for several days before moving on. Each animal may have several nests, which it visits and repairs on a regular cycle. When their bowl-shaped nests stop appearing in the groves and in the forest stands that remain, it can be assumed the aye-aye in the wild is no more. As for any captive-bred animals that may exist, it would hardly make sense to put them back where others have failed to survive. They would die from the same lack of concern, the same indifference to yet another species of animal that has been on the brink since first known to Europeans.

# Pygmy Hippopatamus
## CHOEROPSIS LIBERIENSIS

The pygmy hippopotamus *(Choeropsis liberiensis)* is not a miniature version of the common hippopotamus, as so many people seem to believe. They are structurally quite different animals and don't even belong in the same genus.

The range of the pygmy hippo is strictly West Africa, in dense lowland forests, near fresh water. Countries where there may still be populations are said to be Sierra Leone, Guinea, Liberia, Ivory Coast, and Nigeria. That range, however, is very discontinuous. It is possible to travel in what should be pygmy hippo country for long distances without detecting a trace of the animal. It probably always has been rather sparsely populated even in ideal habitat. Since it is a shy, secretive animal that is both nocturnal and aquatic (although less so than its very much larger cousin), it can be difficult to see. It remains in the most remote, least disturbed areas available and is not a typical roadside animal like so much of Africa's big game. The giant hippo is quite easy to locate and observe, but the pygmy hippo is not, which is why so much less is known about it.

The former sizes of the pygmy hippo population and its range are not known and perhaps never will be, except by supposition. They have been seriously impacted by deforestation, which was inevitable. Their flesh is said to be quite porklike, and they have been heavily hunted. They are still killed by indigenous peoples within the animal's range, without regard for any form of controls.

Without knowing how many there were and where they were to be found, and without firm figures on how many remain and exactly where they might be, it is more than difficult to evaluate their predicament. Because deforestation is going forward at such a devastating rate and because the human population is exploding in Africa, it can be assumed the pygmy hippo is on a collision course with an unkind destiny. Even a pygmy hippo can weigh between five and six hundred pounds. That is all protein, said to be very good protein at that. It is a difficult position for an animal to be in anywhere in the world.

At least 250 pygmy hippos are now being held in seventy-five to eighty zoos, many of which are having breeding successes with the species. That, of course, is all to the good. They make an attractive exhibit although many zoos do not show them to full advantage. It is apparently possible to build captive stocks even further, but what is to become of these animals eventually? It seems likely that they will be a permanent fixture in more and more of the world's zoos while the wild stock continues to decline. There is no suggestion that the human population explosion in Africa will be brought under control in time to prevent permanent habitat degradation, which will be lethal for this retiring species. The demands on tropical forests show no signs of abating, and again that is an impact impossible for this species to tolerate. It is a bad situation all around. The only positive aspect seems to be that the world's zoos, using breeding loans to keep genetic diversity from being lost, can keep the species from becoming extinct, even long after it has vanished in the wild, if indeed that is to be its fate.

The needs of the pygmy hippopotamus are very specialized, a wide variety of plant foods, unpolluted water to retreat to in time of danger, fresh water always at hand, and a reasonable limit on predation by man and animal, not to mention solitude and a limited range of temperature and humidity. That is not a combination of conditions to be found, in all likelihood, outside of the species' native range except in expertly maintained zoo conditions. It appears as if the pygmy hippopotamus will survive in zoos and its natural West African habitat, and nowhere else.

# Grevy Zebra

## EQUUS GREVYI

All of the so-called odd-toed ungulates, the Perissodactyla, are in trouble. What remains of this ancient order includes the equines, the tapirs, and the rhinoceroses—and nothing else. Except for captive-bred and -maintained animals, the entire order could disappear in less than fifty years.

The equines, or equids, include the zebras. One of them, *Equus quagga*, the quagga (pronounced, approximately, *chwagga*) vanished in this century, killed off in its native South Africa. It is now officially listed as extinct. Two of the remaining zebras, the mountain zebra *(E. zebra)* and Hartmann's zebra *(E. z. hartmannae)*, of South and Southwest Africa respectively, are distinctly vulnerable and bear very careful monitoring.

The case is somewhat less clear with one of the most handsome of all modern zebras, *E. grevyi*, the Grevy zebra. It is the largest of the zebras and is distinguished by asslike ears, and pencil-thin stripes that do not go all the way around the body. The belly is white. It has a bristle mane and is impossible to confuse with any other animal, even its zebra cousins. Its normal range has been northern Kenya, Ethiopia, and Somalia. It may be nearing extinction in Somalia but could be in fair-to-good shape in Ethiopia. It is believed that as many as ten thousand specimens may still survive in Kenya north of Mt. Kenya, and they are common in Samburu National Park and its vicinity. They are a great tourist attraction and are not significantly poached. Tourists particularly like them because it is just about impossible to take a bad picture of a Grevy zebra. They are not at all shy once they become accustomed to vehicles, voices, and the whirring and clicking of cameras. The number of tourist dollars even a small band of Grevys is worth to the Kenyan people is hard to estimate, but it is considerable. They are frequently seen in close association with the common zebra, giraffe (in their range, the reticulated giraffe), oryx, and eland. The Grevy, like the common zebra, is an open plains animal and may be mixed in with all kinds of other animals such as impala, ostrich, Grant's gazelle—in fact, the whole parade that makes a "safari" in East Africa such a remarkable experience.

The number of ten thousand surviving animals has been frequently disputed. Whether it is optimistic, pessimistic, or right on the mark is not possible to determine. One of the gravest problems for the species is competition for water and food—the Samburu people, and to a lesser extent other tribes in the northern areas of Kenya, maintain herds of cattle, sheep, goats, camels, and donkeys, and all of them need what the zebra needs. There is constant pressure to keep wild animals away from available water and the best grazing. Although the Grevy will dig for water where that is possible, it is not a substitute for free-range conditions, freedom to move and use what the land has to offer. Organized agriculture is also a problem because it diverts water and reduces the wild animals' options.

The base problem is, of course, human population growth. With Kenya's birth rate at an awesome 8.1 babies per woman, the demands for ever more efficient and ever more preempting agriculture and larger and larger herds of domestic stock are inevitable. Somehow the Grevy zebra and the other water and fodder users are going to have to fit in or vanish. What happened to India is happening to Africa. Human beings are becoming locusts on their own land to their own detriment and that of everything else that lives.

Hundreds of Grevy zebras are now held in the world's zoos and even in private collections. They breed readily in captivity, and the captive herd can be expected to grow. They are as pleasing to zoogoers in their context as the wild specimens are to tourist wildlife buffs.

The needs of wild zebras are well known: space, water, and appropriate grazing. If they are to survive in the wild as one of Africa's most spectacularly decorative animals and a constant drawing card for tourists, all that need be done is allow for those needs. The number of Grevys that live alongside livestock on a private ranch, Lewa Downs, not far from Samburu, proves how easily they fit in when not molested or driven off. It is up to Kenya and Ethiopia. If they want this magnificent species wild on their land, they can have it. No one else can make that determination. One of the world's most exotic animals has the least exotic needs.

# Striped Hyena

## HYAENA HYAENA

There are only four species of hyena left in the world, all in Africa, the Middle East, and Asia. Undoubtedly there were many more forms in the past, but they are gone. The hyenas are known to have flourished in Europe and North America during the Pleistocene. Their range has been contracting and undoubtedly that trend will continue.

The striped hyena *(Hyaena hyaena)* is found in Africa and Asia, in open or rocky country from Senegal and Morocco to Egypt and Tanzania, from Asia Minor and the Arabian Peninsula to southern Soviet Asia and India. That is an enormous area, but the animal is shy and secretive, nowhere densely populated. In some areas, it is endangered; at least some subspecies are. It has suffered like almost all wildlife from habitat loss. It also suffers persecution since it is a predator.

The striped hyena has several unfortunate traits that have not endeared it to man. It is very predatory, in some parts of its range more so than others, and the picture of it as simply a scavenger is an uneducated one at best. It will take live-stock up to and including horses and cattle. It will take fruit and vegetables as well, making it an even worse economic threat. Like man, the species avoids true desert and must be within a reasonable distance of water. That puts man, his gardens, his stock, and the striped hyena in the same general area. But least endearing of all is the fact that the striped hyena will attack human beings, particularly children. There is little love lost on this species.

Still, the hyena has its niche, its place in the evolutionary scheme. Its loss or the loss of any of the four species, would be a serious matter. Hyenas are not dogs. In fact, they are closer to cats than dogs. They probably evolved from the mongoose family, the Viverridae. They are the smallest group within the Carnivora. Among the Carnivora, there are thirty-six species of canines, the Canidae; eight species of bears, the Ursidae; nineteen species in Procyonidae, the raccoons and kin; sixty-four species in Mustelidae, the weasels, badgers, skunks, and otters; seventy species of civets, genets, and mongooses, the Viverridae; thirty-seven species of cat, the Felidae; but just four of the Hyaenidae. It is the smallest group with the heaviest prejudices leveled against it.

One of the hyenas, the aardwolf, has degenerated into an insect-eater with weak jaws that are a threat to no one. The other three, the striped, brown, and spotted (also known as the ''laughing'' hyena and, indeed, it is very vocal) are carnivores, but so are the wild forms of cats and canines. The canines and the wild cats have a great advantage over the hyena. They are frequently quite handsome, some even splendid. Our sense of aesthetics does not cover the hyena, however, and the very name is generally spoken with a degree of disgust. That kind of prejudice has worked very harshly for snakes, a number of the corcodilians, and is working against sharks now, most of which are completely harmless.

The striped hyena can't hide in lakes, rivers, and oceans the way sharks and crocodiles and alligators can. It is far less cryptic than snakes are able to be. It is crepuscular, mainly active at dawn and dusk, or nocturnal, but it can be hunted down, trapped, shot, and poisoned. Life is a harsh reality when a species is dominant and dominating as man turns his hand against an animal, which has no new devices available to it, an animal trapped by its past evolutionary course in a set way of life.

The zoos of the world exhibit hyenas easily. Both the brown hyena and the aardwolf, the two species now listed as rare, are in representative collections. The aardwolf is in about ten zoos, the brown hyena in close to twenty. The full inventory of striped hyena is not kept because it is not yet considered rare because of its enormous range, but seven to ten zoos are breeding them. A worthy task for any zoo is to enlighten the public to the fact that an animal's survival as a species must not ever depend on its publicity or our fictitious perception of it or our evaluation of its life-style. These are disastrously inadequate criteria for anything as basic as survival on the species' one and only planet.

# Chimpanzee

## PAN TROGLODYTES

The chimpanzee *(Pan troglodytes)* is one of the best-known and most beloved of all wild animals. It is, by a wide margin, our own closest living relative. Chimpanzees and gorillas, for example, vary in their genetic material by 13 percent. In contrast, the difference between man and chimpanzee is about 1 percent (everything from 0.5 percent to 5 percent has been estimated for that figure). A chimpanzee, then, is *almost* human—or, if you will, humans are *almost* chimpanzees.

The handbooks on African wildlife give a range for the chimpanzee that is vast and seemingly very encouraging: Senegal, Mali, Gambia, Guinea-Bissau, Guinea, Sierra Leone, Liberia, Ivory Coast, Ghana, Togo, Benin, Nigeria, Cameroon, Rio Muni, Gabon, Cabinda, Central African Republic, Congo (Brazzaville), Zaire, Sudan, Uganda, Rwanda, Burundi, and Tanzania. All of that territory, however, is very misleading. The chimpanzee today, due to many factors, is rare and getting more so all the time. In many of the countries on that list, the chimpanzee population is minuscule, scattered in isolated little bands and rapidly approaching extirpation.

The chimpanzee cannot exist without forests. Perfectly at home on the ground it walks on two or four feet depending on its mood and the conditions it encounters. But it sleeps in trees much of the time, rests in trees, spots danger, and escapes in trees. It does a part of its feeding there as well. It brachiates, or swings arm over arm, often leaping from branch to branch, tree to tree in great athletic sweeps of thirty feet or more. Chimpanzees cannot swim and can only cross small streams by leaping or swinging across in trees. Rivers too broad to cross this way form insurmountable barriers. Chimpanees are active during daylight hours and bed down before sundown in tree nests they make themselves.

Their similarity to human beings has almost been the chimpanzees' undoing. A young chimp today can bring as much as $28,000 on the market, although labs in most parts of the world have agreed not to import any more. Still, the United States government requires by law that certain drugs be tested first on chimpanzees before being released for human use. Each batch must have a chimpanzee test series done first. With AIDS research a matter of extreme urgency, more chimps will be required than ever before. Chimpanzees can contract the AIDS virus, but no chimp yet has become clinical. Chimps apparently don't actually get the disease.

Since they can't import their chimps, the laboratories in countries like the United States that have banned imports from Africa must breed their own. Zoos, too, breed their own chimps. That is far better than the old days when baby chimps were captured and shipped around the world. The capture was effected by shooting the mother out of the trees and taking her baby, if it survived the fall. These assaults seriously disrupted the chimps' complex family life. Other mothers lost their infants, bands became scattered, and some never were able to get back together in their own territory. Many of the chimps died in transit, particularly the very young.

Today, between forty-five and fifty zoos produce baby chimps each year, as do a great many laboratories. Infant survival rate is high and adults with babies make one of the most attractive of all zoo displays. Young chimps have always attracted a great deal of attention as theatrical performers. As fully mature animals, they are usually far too dangerous to handle. A full-grown chimp can weigh as much as 190 ppounds, but is far stronger than several men of that size. Its bite is devastating.

Zoos today are moving their chimpanzees out of the nasty little cages they once used and are putting them on islands behind artificial moats or in natural settings, sometimes held secure behind a single strand of electric fencing and a dry moat.

A new danger to chimps in the wild comes from deforestation. Once the trees are cut down and the botanical diversity of an area is destroyed, the chimps are finished. That factor is pushing the chimps into ever-smaller enclaves, making it more and more difficult for them to establish and maintain territories in a natural way. Chimps are tied to that complex social structure that binds them to each other and can tolerate only a very limited amount of disruption.

Zoos and laboratories have learned a great deal about chimpanzee propagation and about the species' needs in captivity. One thing they are going to have to get much better at is returning chimps to the wild. There have been experiments using islands off the African coast, but so far they have not met with much success. The day is foreseeable when the zoos and the laboratories will be just about the only refuges the chimps have. Some of those captive-born animals could be available for release. Accomplishing that release, however, is a difficult and tricky business.

# Lowland Gorilla

## GORILLA GORILLA

Some animals are obviously critical to our understanding of our world, our evolution, and ourselves. The more like us they are, the easier it is for us to relate to their plight. Although that may not be a scientifically valid way of evaluating other species, it is inevitable. Considerably less like us than the chimpanzees, the gorillas *(Gorilla gorilla)* clearly sound a deep alarm when we look at them and consider their man-caused distress.

There are really three gorillas, two lowland forms, which we will consider here, and the mountain gorilla *(G. g. beringei)*. We will not discuss the mountain subspecies in any detail because there are none in captivity. The general belief is that they would not survive in zoos, or at least none has for long; and none has bred in captivity. Some zoo people feel that, if they had mountain gorillas, with the present level of expertise, those could be maintained and bred as well as the lowland. Still, unless someone is ready to travel far and climb hard jungled slopes for hours, the lowland gorilla is the animal they will come to know.

The gorilla is found only in Equatorial Africa, and in widely separated areas in that vast region. The western lowland *(G. g. gorilla)* is found discontinuously in southeastern Nigeria, southern Cameroon, southwestern Central African Republic, the mainland part of Equatorial Guinea, Gabon, Congo, western Zaire, and a corner of Angola. The eastern lowland gorilla *(G. G. graueri)* is found in Zaire and Uganda. The two lowland populations are at least 1,000 kilometers apart. The rare mountain form is restricted to a range of six extinct volcanos along the Zaire-Uganda-Rwanda border. And that is how much of the world the gorilla has left to it. The list of countries is impressive, but, in fact, only very tiny pockets within those nations are safe gorilla haven. Most of their range is now lost to them, and they keep to ever more restrictive and isolated areas.

Gorillas prefer tropical rain forests. The lowland forms stay pretty much to the territory their name implies, but in some areas have been forced by circumstances to altitudes of six and even seven thousand feet. They are, as has been reported so many times, peaceful vegetarians with a complex social and family life. Although immensely powerful, they seldom do more than intimidate. They seldom have to. They are surprisingly accepting, even trusting animals, and unless molested or assaulted, will allow human beings to come among them and leave in peace. Gorillas that have had bad experiences with human beings, or who are not being accorded the respect they deserve, will flee at the sound, sight, or scent of man.

There are now hundreds of lowland gorillas in well over a hundred zoos. Approximately twenty births are reported a year. A studbook for the world's captive population is maintained at the zoo in Frankfurt-am-Main, Germany.

Gorillas are not the easiest of zoo animals to maintain. They require special conditions to be humanely kept, including isolation from human beings to avoid respiratory infections as well as a complex diet including a variety of fruits and vegetables along with supplements. They are immensely powerful and have the capacity to do enormous damage to their display and their keepers, more out of boredom, perhaps, than out of any kind of malice. A gorilla display that protects both the animals and the public, that has educational value, that is properly attuned to the local climate (these are, after all, equatorial animals), that is considerate of these highly intelligent animals' emotional needs, and yet encourages natural group living and reproduction, is a major capital undertaking for any zoo. Enough zoos have accomplished these goals, however, not to allow for any excuses from those that have not. No zoo has the right to display gorillas unless it can do so properly.

The gorilla, one of the most fascinating of all animal species, is safe in the world's zoo collections, yet subject to the whims and fancies of often unstable political units in the wild. How these two facts can work on or for each other is not clear. Until such a terribly complex matter can be sorted out, the zoos must do what they have been doing: protecting the gorillas that are born to their collections to the best of their ability. Any findings or propaganda that can be fed back to the gorillas' places of origin to encourage conservation efforts there could make an extremely important difference.

# White Rhinoceros

## CERATOTHERIUM SIMUM

The massive rhinoceroses once ranged, in many species and genera now extinct, over most of Africa south of the Sahara, perhaps in North Africa as well, and in both south-central and southeastern Asia. Of what was once a rich variety of animals, only five species in four genera have survived into our time. Four of these species are endangered: the African black or prehensile-lipped, the Sumatran or hairy, the Asian one-horned, and the Indian. The African square-lipped or white rhinoceros *(Ceratotherium simum)* alone seems to be relatively safe, at least for the time being.

Except for the elephants, both African and Asian, and the hippopotamus, the white rhino is the largest of all surviving land animals. A large specimen can weigh up to eight thousand pounds.

As recently as two thousand years ago, the white rhino (it is just about the same color as the African black rhino, a shade of gray) ranged over a vast area, all the way up the Nile Valley into Egypt and probably over across much of northwestern Africa. Early in this century, they were found in Chad, the Central Africa Republic, the Sudan, Zaire, and parts of Uganda and Kenya as well as the southern subspecies in Angola, and probably Zambia, Mozambique, Rhodesia, Botswana, Namibia, and South Africa. The northern animals are probably just about gone. Only a small part of the southern form's range is available to them, but within parks and reserves, they are apparently well enough protected. Africa is an insecure home for any wild species because of impending political shifts and upheavals, but as long as the immediate problems of poaching and habitat degradation are under control, at least in the south, optimism is in order.

The white rhino is, unlike the other rhinoceros, strictly a grazing animal and lives in a parklike savanna country. White rhinos prefer to be near trees for shade and water. They are more gregarious than the other rhinoceros and are less suspicious and more easygoing as well. They are often seen in groups of up to six animals. When confined to parks and preserves, the groups can appear to be larger but probably are not naturally so.

In recent years, efforts were made to transplant surplus animals from southern populations into the former range of the northern subspecies *(C. s. cottoni)*. They were even assigned armed wardens to guard them during the day when they were out grazing. In some places, they were taken in at night in an effort to provide maximum protection. The rhino shown in this photo, taken a few years ago, is one of such a group. Unfortunately, this experiment failed, not because the southern animals could not adjust to their northern cousin's habitats but because human predators were too voracious. The transplants were killed off by poachers no matter how sincere the efforts to secure their newly assigned range. The black rhinoceros is already severely pressed by tribesmen filtering south from Somalia in search of the huge earnings to be had with rhino horn exported to Asia. Thus it is unlikely that further efforts to move white rhinoceros north to experience the same ill fate will be made. There isn't much point to it.

White rhinoceros do very well in zoos because they are peaceful, sensible giants that settle down quickly. They are in at least 120 zoos and number in the hundreds in the census. They breed readily, although the number produced is not great. They provide an interesting zoo display especially when exhibited in a large, natural parklike area. Other mammals and birds can be displayed with them without problem. The efforts to save them in southern Africa, and the success of those efforts, provide a good success story in an ongoing adventure that is far too often wholly negative.

It would be possible to repopulate much of the former white rhinoceros range with zoo animals and with animals from the parks in the southern one-third of Africa if northern areas could ever be made secure. The market for rhino horn and skin will have to be eradicated in Asia, and it is not yet clear how that can be done. Everything from dehorning rhinos in the wild to spreading the word among Muslim customers that science has determined the rhino is a kind of pig (which it is not!) have been proposed, and in some instances tried. Nothing yet has worked. In time, surely, something will.

# Scimitar-Horned Oryx

ORYX DAMMAH

The oryx are represented by three species, all of one genus, all from Africa. The scimitar-horned oryx *(Oryx dammah)* is one of the two northern species, originally ranging from Morocco and Senegal to Egypt and the Sudan and possibly over into Israel and other Middle East states. It is an animal of arid and semiarid plains, somehow managing despite its size to survive on the sparse vegetation found in those regions. They weigh from four to almost five hundred pounds, and are over five feet at the shoulder. When water is available they utilize it, but when it is not, they can subsist for long periods, getting the moisture they need from wild melons, plant bulbs, and other plant material. They are very well adapted to dry country. What we would consider a harsh environment is not harsh for them. It was what they were evolved to deal with, and they do it without stress.

One distinctive feature of the scimitar-horned oryx is their horns, which, unlike the horns of the other two species, are curved. They can be almost five feet long and can be tough on predators, but are useless against man.

And the species' problems have come from man. Huge flocks and herds of livestock have been driven to consume whatever water has been available and to nibble down all available plant life to useless stubs. When goats and sheep have worked through an area in large numbers, there is nothing left for wildlife. Another factor has been hunting to an unconscionable level with every mode of transportation from aircraft to air-conditioned limousines as well as every imaginable form of hunting and military armament. The species has crumbled before the dual onslaught.

There are no meaningful numbers for original populations, but it is believed that over the large areas inhabited by these hardy animals, there were tens of thousands. Today only hundreds survive in the wild.

At any one time, there are between six and eight hundred scimitar-horned oryx in captivity, with all of them presumed to be captive bred. A couple of hundred are born in captivity every year at least. The Nature Reserves Authority in Israel has made the species one of its prime projects, and the animals are reproducing well in wild but fenced reserve land. Whether or not the species actually did reach Israel is not argued. It is a species typical to the region and perhaps did overlap the range of the Arabian oryx *(O. leucoryx),* which is known to have ranged there and which is also a major project in Israel.

If and when habitat is secured from all hunting and from the overwhelming presence of livestock en masse, the zoos of the world have the reservoir that could be used to restock animals where they originally roamed. Without man-related stress, the species could probably recover until it again reached large herds. The scimitar-horned oryx is a gregarious animal and is found normally in bands or herds of twenty to forty individuals. It is reported that when there has been surface water, or during migrations, as many as a thousand animals might be seen together. All of the oryx are gregarious to some degree, but the scimitar-horned even more than the others.

Fortunately the oryx, large and robust antelope that they are, can fare well in captivity and can function perfectly well when reintroduced to an area natural for them where their needs can be met. They do not have to learn from their parents how to hunt, for their prey is what grows where they naturally wander. Far more of what they have to know comes in their genetic package than is the case with predators, in which there are long learning periods. Hoofed animals are born far more precocious than their predators and that makes reintroduction simpler. The more time the young of a species must spend in the care of their mother, or both parents, the more difficult it is to return them to the wild. The scimitar-horned oryx is a perfect candidate for release when the politics, ethics, and sociology of man permit it.

# Somali Wild Ass

## EQUUS AFRICANUS SOMALICUS

It is not clear exactly what the proper scientific name is for this animal, but the Somali wild ass may be a subspecies of the African wild ass, in which case *Equus africanus somalicus* is probably a safe guess. The importance of proper identification comes when former and present ranges are being analyzed and when the status of species is being determined. It is generally believed that this form is the true ancestor of the domestic donkey, and therefore mules as well. It is a swift, tough animal that is highly social with its own kind, even if fights are common, particularly among males. Males guard their herds or harems jealously. Any young males that try to move in on the old jack or stallion's holdings will have to fight, sometimes to the death. The males can be extremely rough during mating, and there has been at least one case where a stallion killed a mare during mating, a tragic loss for the captive herd. All wild equines, asses, wild and even feral horses, and zebras are extremely rugged animals. They lash out with their hind feet, rear, and use their front feet like pile drivers. They bite, often with terrible effect, at the least provocation. They are built for speed, but when it is time to stand and fight, they are more than capable of taking the challenge.

The Somali wild ass, as its name implies, is found in Somalia and Ethiopia. It once ranged much farther than that, and it was no doubt one of the animals referred to in the Bible. Because of that the Nature Reserves Authority in Israel has established carefully monitored herds at Hai-Bar and elsewhere. It is probably one of the very few places on earth (and possibly the only one) where this animal can range where it originally ranged and not be in danger of being shot. These animals are, of course, strictly protected in Israel, and no one is allowed to disturb them for any reason. They are not being handled or manipulated so much that they will lose their natural wild instincts and capabilities.

Several things contributed to the decimation of the original populations of this species. War, no stranger to the Middle East and North Africa, particularly early in this century, raised havoc with the shy animals. They were driven from areas where they could feed and find water. Bored soldiers shot them for no reason at all. Family groups were split by the unfamiliar intrusions, and young were lost. Native peoples have also hunted the Somali wild ass for their skins and meat, but not just to eat. Two tribes at least, the Somalis and the Afar, use the meat and fat of this wild equid for medicine. There has been, too, habitat degradation and competition with livestock for grazing and water. Then there has been the old enemy, hybridization. Some of the wild animals mated with domestic donkeys that had gone wild or were put out to graze until needed again. Even though the domestic animals almost certainly did descend from the wild ass centuries ago, enough changes have occurred to make a cross-back foal a hybrid.

In normal years, the attrition from hunting could be tolerated. But when drought years hit, the combination of forces working against the shrinking herds was devastating. Gestation for the species is thirteen months. Foals are weaned normally at four months and mature at two years. The foal has to be able to accompany its mother as she moves around for food and water within an hour of its birth. If it can't, it almost certainly will not survive the tough life it is destined to lead. At a few days of age, mother and foal move back into the herd, which means it already is fast on its feet. Both young and adults must drink every two or three days. They inhabit semiarid regions far from human beings.

There are generally forty to fifty Somali wild ass held in eight to ten of the world's zoos. Five or six institutions generally report breeding successes every year, including the wild but controlled herd at Hai-Bar. This is a species that is rare and probably getting even more rare in the wild. It probably can stand translocation if the problems of parasites can be solved. The wild animals generally carry parasitic flukes, which makes it difficult to get permission to move them from country to country.

Captive propagation will play an important role in saving this handsome and historically important species from extinction. If their old range can ever be made secure for them, even in part, they could readily be released in the wild, particularly small herds that had been allowed to form while still in captivity. Like all social animals everything for them goes much better if a hierarchy is in place.

# Dorcas Gazelle

## GAZELLA DORCAS

The handsome little dorcas gazelle *(Gazella dorcas),* up to twenty-six inches at the shoulder and fifty-five pounds, once ranged widely from Israel, Syria, and Arabia across North Africa from Eritrea and Egypt west to Morocco and Mauritania. It inhabited numerous valleys in the Sahara Desert. Almost all of that is now history.

The dorcas gazelle is rare to nonexistent any place outside of Israel, where it is called the Negev gazelle. In Israel, this gazelle is found free-roaming from the Judaean Desert and the northwestern part of the Negev south and is in good numbers within Hai-Bar. It is estimated that the herds total about a thousand animals.

The survey of the subspecies of the dorcas published in 1972 by the International Union for the Conservation of Nature and Natural Resources was not encouraging. Of the Moroccan dorcas gazelle *(G. d. massaesyla)* it said, "Endangered; overhunting has greatly reduced its numbers, and overgrazing by domestic livestock has destroyed much of its range." Of the Saudi Arabian dorcas gazelle *(G. d. saudiya),* "Endangered; population throughout much of its extensive range greatly depleted by *mechanized hunting* but has increased in Israel." On Pelzeln's gazelle *(G. d. pelzelni)* found in Somalia, "Endangered as a result of excessive hunting and serious overgrazing by domestic livestock."

A very serious problem arose for all hoofed wildlife in North Africa and the Middle East after World War II. There were many jeeps and other vehicles and weapons left over and either abandoned or sold off by departing armies or middlemen. This hardware came into the hands of sheiks, who developed a sporting game for visiting dignitaries. Spotter planes went ahead and reported the whereabouts of herds of gazelle and larger antelope like the Arabian and Saharan oryx to radio-equipped air-conditioned Cadillacs that were accompanied by Jeeps and other vehicles with machine guns mounted to fire over the windshield. If necessary, the planes would drive the animals toward a rendezvous and just before the meeting, the hunters would change over to the Jeeps, and when they met the herds rake them with the automatic weapons. That is at least one definition of "overhunting."

Since the small gazelles lived exclusively in areas where water and grazing are both at a premium, competition with livestock attended by jealous herdsmen made it impossible to survive even if they escaped the machine-gun-equipped hunters. It was clear that they would go, and apparently they did, although many of the areas they inhabited are still so extremely remote, some small numbers may have survived. It is doubtful, however.

Eight to ten zoos regularly report births, and the number of animals in captivity is between 150 and two hundred animals, all in four or five collections. At least half of that number are being held on the ranges at Hai-Bar. All the animals are presumed to be captive bred, and except for the preserve, there is no other probable source for new genetic material. There are enough, however, that zoos in suitable climates with enough room for the animals to reproduce could make the species self-sustaining. It might be possible to return stock, although probably not of the former subspecies, to places where the dorcas once roamed in herds of up to sixty animals. Before that is done, however, the people in those areas are going to have to take wildlife conservation much more seriously.

This is a case where animals, whole subspecies, were apparently destroyed in orgies of killing. That is not a combination any animal is likely to be able to withstand. Fortunately, in captivity, there is the stock to put at least one subspecies back on the track to recovery.

# Saddlebill Stork

## EPHIPPIORHYNCHUS SENEGALENSIS

When most people think of Africa, they think of its incredible mammals, lion, cheetah and leopard, rhino, hippo and elephant, gorilla and chimpanzee. But when birdwatchers think of Africa, their eyes get that faraway dream quality of people on a trip of fancy.

Africa is the most incredible of all continents for seeing birds in their absolutely unbelievable variety. A few countries in South America, such as Colombia, may have a greater number of species than a bird paradise such as Kenya, but the open savanna country of much of Africa allows birds to be seen; whereas, many of Colombia's treasures are under a thick canopy and are seldom seen except by the most persistent.

A prime example of Africa's spectacular bird life is the saddlebill stork, or jabiru *(Ephippiorhynchus senegalensis)*. Sixty-five or more inches in length, this giant has black and white plumage, like most storks, and a massive red and black bill with a yellow saddle across its base. The sexes are the same, except the male has brown eyes while the female's are yellow. This species is a favorite with newcomers to Africa, fortunate to see it. The variety of birds is so bewildering, they often have trouble making a positive identification, but the ostrich and the spectacular saddlebill stork are sure-fire "positives" every time.

The range, on paper, is huge for this species. It is widely distributed on the continent except in Somalia and in the extreme south. It is not seen in large numbers anywhere and a traveler can go weeks without seeing even one of them. They are generally found along the larger rivers, in swamps and marshes and around lakes. They are stately and magnificent as they stride through or near shallow water, constantly seeking prey. They feed on fish, amphibians, and some reptiles. Undoubtedly, insects such as large grasshoppers and locusts, and perhaps also mollusks, form a part of their prey. They take much of their food on land near water and not just in the water itself. They are seen elsewhere in the wild when in transit. Like most storks they are powerful fliers and great soarers.

Because they do live only near water, in captivity, they require a fairly large open area and a place literally to stretch their legs. They are not often seen in captivity except in the better-endowed and the highly specialized collections, although they provide a stunning display. Often they are in enclosures with other birds from the same continent and can be exhibited with gazelles and antelope. Animals displayed in natural groupings give zoo visitors a truer sense of the biological diversity the animals represent. This is far and away the best way to exhibit animals.

Not everything the saddlebill stork eats in the wild is known. Nor are the chemicals it may get from mineral-rich soils and even highly selective plant elements understood so the diet of these birds in captivity is complex and expensive. The saddlebill stork may not be an ideal bird for small zoos with a very limited amount of space to devote to birds of this size, or without the necessary money for their proper care. No zoo should possess so much as a single animal it cannot provide with its true needs, including space.

The saddlebill apparently does not easily breed in captivity, and it cannot be classified as really rare in the wild. Unlike land animals, these powerful fliers can move over great distances in a relatively short time and get to suitable habitat when there is drought or when other factors drive them off. It is very difficult to estimate a true status for them on the survival scale, but they seem to be safe at the moment. Still, the world has been shrinking for birds as large and specialized as this one. There were once many more forms than there are now. The problem today is to be certain that the ones that survive don't follow their ancestral forms into oblivion. As a species, the saddlebill stork is not really more important than any other kind of bird, but looking at this one in the Los Angeles Zoo, it can be difficult to accept that fact. It looks important in a special kind of way.

# Pink Pigeon

## COLUMBA MAYERI

The pigeons and doves (the words are really interchangeable) are a widely dispersed, highly successful group of over 280 species. The forty genera contain birds that range in size from about that of a hen turkey to a lark. The birds are found feeding and nesting in large cities. on farms, in jungles, on cliffs, on the ground, and at the snow line. There is almost no habitat one pigeon or another can't utilize at least part of the time.

The genus *Columba* contains at least fifty species ranging from the incredibly adaptable and familiar rock dove *(C. livia)* (the pigeon of city parks all around the world) to the rare and seriously endangered Mauritius pigeon, also known as the pink pigeon *(C. mayeri),* and the chestnut-tailed pigeon. Given foreign-language names (*pigeons des mares,* for example) the species has almost as many names as there are free-living specimens.

Not very much is known about this species in the wild except that it has apparently always been limited to Mauritius east of Madagascar in the Indian Ocean. Even on that island, living specimens are limited to only the most remote forests in the area known as the Southwestern Plateau. They are apparently nowhere near as adaptable as their cogenitor *livia.*

Like their relative, however, they are apparently quite tame and trusting and do not like the high forest trees. Their flight is not as spectacular as that of the common rock dove, and they never seem to fly very high, very fast, or very far. Little is known of their feeding or nesting habits in the wild. They behave very much like the rock dove at mating time, and the similarities have often been recorded.

It is quite likely that there are no more than twenty or so of these birds left in the wild, which makes the species one of the most endangered in the world. Left alone, it would almost certainly become extinct. There is the always present problem of deforestation, and twenty birds provide far too narrow a genetic base for the species to retain vigor. It is impossible to say where the break point is, but twenty birds certainly is below it. The species would be doomed were it not for captive propagation.

In 1976, Gerald Durrell of the Jersey Wildlife Preservation Trust became interested in the species and began a breeding program at his rare-animal compound on the Island of Jersey.

There are a few American zoos as well with an active program with the species, and some have already been placed back in the wild on Mauritius.

The release of captives is an expensive affair with a very high measure of risk involved. The animals have to be transported to often remote areas and then turned loose in sites carefully chosen for what might be the deceptive appearance of being intact. For a species really to fit back in, the whole ecosystem must contain many if not all of its original elements. Food and nesting sites must be available, water as per the needs of each species, predators must be present only in normal numbers, and no exotic predators or competitors can have been introduced in most instances. That is often one of the most difficult problems since even livestock, sheep, goats, pigs, and pariahs like rats, feral cats, and dogs can all be serious predators or serious competitors.

Then there is the question of reproduction. Will the captive-bred and recently released animals breed and successfully raise their young? That is always an unknown factor. What animals eventually were coaxed to do in an ideal captive situation may not hold true once they are on their own. It is, or at least can be, very expensive to monitor the animals once they are back in the wild unless highly intelligent and really committed local help can be enlisted. There is, too, the problem of habitat security. What guarantees are there that the factors that endangered the species in the first place are not still present and won't make the lives of the returnees uncertain as well?

There is the virtually always unknown factor of population dynamics. That is the break point referred to earlier. How many specimens must there be for the species to continue to try to exist? How important is competition among males, and how important is the selectivity of the females? If there are too few of either sex to choose from, the animals may not breed at all. It would be as if they simply had lost interest in existing as a species any longer.

As for the fate of the pink pigeon of Mauritius, the jury is still out. If it has been too soon to know how the released captive-bred birds are faring there are ever-increasing numbers in captivity and perhaps sometime in the future, the experiment can be tried again.

# Waldrapp Ibis

## GERONTICUS EREMITA

The not terribly pretty (prettiness is not a criterion for survival, fortunately) Waldrapp ibis *(Geronticus eremita)* is one of the world's most seriously endangered birds in the wild. It also has an unpleasant odor. As recently as the seventeenth century, the Waldrapp was widely distributed in at least southern Europe, but it has been several hundred years since any have been seen there, except the captive birds of Gerald Durell on the Island of Jersey, and in recent years, the relatively small number in about twenty-five other European zoos and collections. There have been a few in zoos in Japan and the United States as well.

The Waldrapp, also known as the red-cheeked and hermit, ibis is a bird of dry country, feeding for the most part on beetles. It is a cliff and colonial nester, wherever a remnant population might exist. The last known specimens in western Asia were reported from Turkey, but that population suffered the same fate as the one in Europe: habitat and food loss leading to extinction, or at least extirpation in a region. It has been a downhill course for the species since the 1600s.

The only birds still in the wild are probably in Morocco. Captive-breeding plans offer the only hope the species has. Relatively few studbooks are kept for birds, but one is maintained at Adenau, Germany. If present plans move ahead, the four or five hundred specimens in zoos will be bred up to a much more substantial and certainly more secure number, and the trip back to Morocco, at least, will begin.

Morocco is reportedly building enclosures to receive the captive-bred birds and will launch a breeding program there. Eventually the birds will be released back into the wild in selected parks and preserves. If all of this works in Morocco, perhaps other parts of North Africa could accept the species, too. Then the eastern end of the Mediterranean and, although it is little more than a dream now, Europe. As a result of all of the hard work and expense and the expertise developed in zoos around the world, another species may not only survive into another century but do so in the wild with at least some in areas where they have not been seen in living memory.

If the zoos can have a finest hour, it would be this or one like it. Not only did they take the responsibility for a species very nearly extinct in the wild but they did so with a species that can hardly be considered a major attraction for the general public. There was, then, no real economic impetus. Then they developed the avicultural sophistication to bring the bird back up in numbers, and to maintain a studbook to avoid a narrow genetic pool in any one institution; and then they convinced a country with a great many other problems to show significant concern for an evil-smelling and far-from-attractive bird of no economic importance, not even for tourism. It is the kind of rescue effort that only a number of zoos from a number of different parts of the world working together could have accomplished. Though not the first such story, it does demonstrate what can be done when the will to rescue a species is coupled with the means (the money!) to do it and the cooperation of a country upon whom the success of the venture must eventually rest.

The question must be asked, For how many species can this kind of effort be expended? It certainly can't be done for a very large percentage of the world's threatened and endangered species, probably not at all for invertebrates. When it comes to reptiles, birds, and mammals, how are choices to be made?

Clearly if one major zoo director takes on a species as a personal challenge, he or she will find peers to help. But what of species without personal champions? There eventually will have to be criteria. But even when they exist, what authority is there to get hundreds of institutions in dozens of countries to accept or comply? For the moment, the Waldrapp ibis can be said to be on a list of the very lucky. For the other species in dire trouble, it still is a matter of chance.

# Pangolin

## MANIS TETRADACTYLA

The pangolins are a strange group of animals, off in an order of their own, Pholidota. There is just one family, just a single genus with seven species. They range widely over Africa and Asia, from West Africa to Sri Lanka, Taiwan and Sumatra, Java, Borneo and Palawan. Their distinctive scales are attached to their tough skin. One easy way to determine if a specimen is Asian or African is to examine the scales. In the Asian species, there are several hairs at the base of each scale; the hairs are lacking in the African species. Four out of the seven species come from Africa.

The specimen shown here in the Los Angeles Zoo is believed to be the West African long-tailed (*Manis tetradactyla*, sometimes *M. longicaudata*). It has had a strange history. It apparently was a stowaway on a cargo plane that was loaded in Lagos, Nigeria, and carried to Amsterdam where it was still not detected. The plane then flew on to Los Angeles and the animal, alive and well, was discovered. U.S. authorities turned it over to the Los Angeles Zoo for temporary safekeeping, but papers are in the works as of this writing to consign it to the zoo on a permanent basis. It is a young animal, apparently, but unfortunately the group to which it belongs has not done well in captivity. Lacking experience, zoos don't know very much about them. It refused all food at first, but is now eating an anteater diet. Unfortunately, this specimen is the only one of its kind in the United States. It may in fact be the only one in captivity anywhere. It is the kind of animal where there are many more questions than answers.

At one time, the seven pangolins were assigned to an entirely different order, Edentata. That put them together with the sloths, anteaters, armadillos, and aardvark. It was decided in time that while all of those animals had termites and ants as part or all of their regular diet, they weren't really down from the same ancestors. The pangolins were set apart still without much real knowledge available that could be helpful to zoos wanting to hold them and breed them.

The status of the pangolins in the wild is also imperfectly understood. At least one African species, Temminck's ground pangolin, is listed as endangered. Throughout their range, apparently, all species are taken by native people for food. They are said to provide very palatable meat. In Asia, pangolin scales are said to be good medicine for everything from venereal disease to skin disorders. Salves, as well as internal medicines, are made from ground-up pangolin scales. This, of course, impacts very harshly on the animals. It is known that between 1958 and 1964, over sixty tons of pangolin scales were exported from Sarawak alone in perfectly legal transactions. That represented an estimated fifty thousand animals. It is believed that most or perhaps all of the scales went to China where everything from rhinoceros horn to bear's paws are ground up and used for medications without the existence of a shred of evidence that any of it does any good. The same kind of appalling consumption occurs in Japan.

It is one thing to get sports hunters to ease off on a species in trouble, and people will even take to eating different meats, wild or domestic, for the same reason, but it is another problem altogether to get tradition-bound people to alter their pharmacological beliefs. They come from far back and have unquestioned currency. If a woman thinks a pinch of rhino horn will cure her infant of a high fever, she is going to see a traditional medicine source and buy rhino horn. The same is true, of course, of pangolin scales. And such beliefs are not limited to ignorant, backward segments of a population. In downtown Tokyo, in an area where people are carrying Gucci attaché cases and wearing expensive hi-tech watches, there are medicine shops with gleaming brass and glass fixtures and display cases selling seal penises steeped in alcohol and other natural atrocities. It is an ironic twist in the fate of wildlife.

There is little evidence yet that the zoos of the world can do much to help the seven pangolin species of the world. If that does not change, and a single specimen in the entire Western Hemisphere, does not offer much encouragement, the pangolins could go. In fact, it seems almost an inevitability.

# Radiated Tortoise

## GEOCHELONE RADIATA

The order Testudines, encompassing as it does the tortoises and turtles, represents some of the most vulnerable creatures left on earth. The sea turtles vanish if their traditional egg-laying beaches are preempted for human use or if they are overhunted for meat. Bog, mud, stream, and pond turtles vanish if their habitat, a very fragile one at that, is drained, seriously disrupted, or badly polluted. All continental species—that is, all but the oceanic turtles—are heavily impacted by automobiles and other vehicles, both on- and off-road varieties.

No group is more vulnerable, though, than the tortoises. They are generally very slow-moving and highly visible land animals with no way of escaping or protecting themselves except for hiding. And once they have been spotted, hiding usually doesn't work. Those that either burrow themselves or use the burrows of other animals may hide for a time but sooner or later they have to show themselves to mate, to eat, and to move to fresh, more profitable habitat. They cannot hide underground indefinitely. Then, too, they are egg-layers and their young go through two phases of vulnerability. Their eggs are taken by a wide variety of other reptiles, by birds if the eggs are exposed, and by small mammals. After the eggs hatch, the small tortoises are again easy prey for many animals and they, too, must sooner or later move around to satisfy basic needs and in so doing expose themselves.

The only reason the tortoises have been able to last this long is their slow metabolism. They don't have to eat as often as many other animals, or drink if they drink at all. They can wait out bad weather, and they can go to ground in case of brush and grass fires. They can last in hiding longer than most other animals could survive. But there are factors that even the slow, patient tortoise cannot outlast.

On Madagascar, it should come as a surprise to no one, there is a tortoise in trouble. The handsome radiated tortoise (*Testudo* or, probably, *Geochelone radiata*) is from the south and southwest of the island. In the seventeenth century, it was used as medicine although details of just how it was used and what it was supposed to do are sparse. They may be pretty much a thing of the past although one could speculate that any tortoises reaching China or Japan (Hong Kong, Taiwan, Macao, and Singapore included, of course) might

well end up in a native herbal pharmacy. Most parts of most animals, it is claimed, aid in fertility problems and pediatric nocturnal fevers.

There are reports that some native peoples on Madagascar also eat the radiated tortoise although it is not clear how heavily that impacts the population. Although the tortoise is strictly protected and is supposed to be left in peace, two export industries have existed at least until very recently, and it is reasonable to suspect some smuggling is still going on. They have been attractive animals in the pet trade and a good many have gone to the United States and Europe for turtle fanciers. It is ironic that a great many people who are fond enough of turtles and tortoises to raise them and belong to turtle/tortoise clubs and societies have been a major cause of their demise in the wild by providing a ready market for hijacked individuals. Many collectors and fanciers decry the practice, of course, and there are good conservationists in the turtle/tortoise fancy. Still, a lot of wild populations have been seriously reduced to satisfy the people who claim to love them most.

The second illegal export trade has been to supply tortoises to the food market. They have been sent to the island of Reunion for that purpose. The Chinese are known to favor tortoise meat with no questions asked as to the source or the condition of the wild populations. How effective the ban has been is not known.

The radiated tortoise does well in captivity. There are generally between 150 and two hundred in zoos (and they, like all tortoises, are long-lived) in forty to fifty collections. Of course, that listing does not include unregistered private collections where the animals may be kept legally or illegally. In some instances, they may exist but be misidentified. A small number of legal collections, zoos for the most part, have been successfully breeding the species, and the eggs have hatched. Hatching is still an exciting event when it happens, but there are probably enough captive animals so that some reintroduction program could be launched if a suitable area were known to be secure on their native island. It is fortunate that tortoises "store" well and live long lives. The zoos and better private collections can go far with this species. The rest is up to the government on Madagascar.

# Parson's Chameleon

## CHAMAELEO PARSONII

The giant island of Madagascar was probably once a part of Africa, although there should be some hesitancy about making it sound like a proven fact. The life on the island is a strange mixture. Of the ninety-seven species of ebony found on the island, only one species is found anywhere else in the world. There are 130 species of palm tree on Madagascar, only two of which appear anywhere else. There are 1,024 species of beetle and 942 of them are endemic, exclusive to the one land mass.

There are animals on the island, the fourth largest in the world, that are distinctly African in type. Among them is a group of spectacular lizards, the chameleons, family Chamaelontidae. Two thirds of the world's chameleons are found only on the island and that includes the smallest land vertebrate known, *Brookesia minima.*

Parson's chameleon *(Chamaeleo parsonii)* pictured here is one those beautiful and intriguing species peculiar to the island that may soon be in desperate trouble if, indeed, is not already. Chameleons are creatures of trees and bushes and cannot survive when they are deprived of them, as means of concealment if for no other reason. There is so much deforestation on Madagascar—for the wonderful tropical hardwoods such as ebony and to make room for more and more agriculture—that species are being felled almost as fast as the trees are. In the small enclaves of trees and brush left, the isolation of animals like chameleons becomes progressively more destructive. Snakes, birds, and small mammalian predators like the fossa have been easy pickings for as long as they themselves last. In the long term, they too will be eliminated by the random clear-cutting that is taking place. It is ironic that when a forest in Madagascar is demolished to make room for agriculture, the land will be productive for only two or three years, and then the farmers have to clear more forest. It will be at least eighty to a hundred years before anything resembling the forest will regrow.

There is a prejudice against chameleons among native people in Africa as well as on Madagascar that harks back to mythology. During a time of great drought, the people decided to send a messenger to the gods to tell them how bad things were, how all of the people would soon die of starvation unless the gods sent rain. They chose a chameleon to make the trip, but the lizard moves so slowly that by the time the messenger got to the gods it was too late. The people of Madagascar and Africa generally do not like chameleons and very little sympathy can be expected for their plight.

Although there are Parson's chameleons in zoos around the world, the species so far has resisted all attempts to breed them and rear them successfully. In the United States, institutions in Houston, Cincinnati, and Oklahoma City are among those with Parson's in their collections. There is the general feeling that sooner or later these live-bearers (many reptiles, of course, are egg layers) will reproduce in captivity. It may soon be a matter of some considerable concern because the unique system of Madagascar is imploding on all levels. The very much smaller animals, invertebrates, and many of the smaller plant forms are disappearing at an accelerating rate. Many have gone and many will go without ever having been identified. Without even being named, much less studied, there is no way of determining what all of the interrelationships are, how lemurs, aye-aye, chameleons, trees, bushes, and smaller flowering plants all interact. In whatever future this planet, indeed this cosmos might have, it is almost certainly a fact that a mixture of life such as that once found and to some extent still found on Madagascar could never come into being again. The wondrous-looking Parson's chameleon is only a single example of a silent, retiring animal that represents all the rest.

# EUROPE/ASIA/AUSTRO-PACIFIC

# Babirusa

BABYROUSA BABYRUSSA

Fortunately for the 225-pound babirusa *(Babyrousa baby-rousa),* man was not evolved on this planet to evaluate its other species of animals aesthetically but rather to protect biological diversity in any form it can be found. The babirusa is a loose-skinned, unlovely member of the family Suidae, the true swine. With four tusks, two of them growing up through the top of the muzzle, it differs from other wild pigs in which the tusks grow out to the side and then up. Its lower tusks are dangerous daggers when the animal is in combat. Although it has a distinctly piglike snout, it does not appear to root as other members of the family do. It lives on fruit that has fallen from trees and bushes and almost certainly relies on foliage as well. Its habitats are moist forests and canebrakes along the shores of rivers and lakes. It is very fast on its feet. A powerful swimmer, it negotiates seawater as well as fresh. It is known to have moved from island to island in search of undisturbed habitat and to keep from overpopulating an area where young have been produced over a period of time. Like so much of today's wildlife, it is fighting a never-ending battle to reduce the pressure it feels from several sources.

The extent of the original range of the babirusa is not known for certain. It most likely included the Celebes, the Togian and Sulu Islands, and at least Bulu Island in the Moluccas, with the Buru and Sulu Island populations probably the result of human introduction. Native peoples hunt the babirusa for food by driving them into nets strung out on poles. Since babirusa generally travel in small sounders, or parties, a number can be captured in a relatively simple organized drive. The young animals are frequently taken and raised in villages where they are easily trained and maintained.

Constant pressure on wild populations has reduced the babirusa's numbers to what are dangerously low levels in some areas. Add to that unrelenting hunting, human population growth, and deforestation, and the babirusa can be reckoned in harm's way. It is one of only eight species left in the true wild swine family.

There is a great deal of lore surrounding this animal, no doubt due to the experience natives have had keeping it in captivity and its value as a food source. Natives say it uses its four upward trained tusks to hang from trees at night. In fact the babirusa in the wild is, if anything, more active at night than in the daylight hours, particularly in areas where there is heavy human activity. Natives also say its tusks are like a deer's antlers and presumably shed, which is not true. There are tales, too, of the medicinal value as well as the food value of the babirusa as well as many other stories— few if any based on fact. The babirusa is a large, conspicuous animal that has figured prominently in the life-style of the people who share or live adjacent to its habitat.

The babirusa does quite well in captivity with specimens on record as having survived for as long as twenty-four years. Anywhere from fifty to a hundred babirusa may be living in zoos at any one time and a few are born in collections every year. Their litters are small, usually only two young after a gestation period of 125 to 150 days. The females have only two pairs of nipples. There are restrictions on the shipment and importation of members of the swine family, in the United States at least, so it is unlikely that this species can be as widely distributed in the world's major zoological collections as so many other species of troubled wildlife can be.

The pig has played an enormously important role in the rise of animal husbandry and in the settled rather than nomadic life of man. Although the babirusa is probably not the pig's direct ancestor, it would be a singular loss for any wild member of the swine family to vanish. The eight remaining species represent biological diversity of immeasurable value and historic interest. There are plenty of Asian domestic swine varieties to supply even remote human populations with all the pig meat they need.

# Przewalski Horse

## EQUUS PRZEWALSKII

The Przewalski (pronounced *shah-walski*), or Mongolian wild horse *(Equus przewalskii)*, is the only true wild horse left on earth. The tarpon, the only other wild species to survive into modern times, died out in the 1860s in Hungary. The tarpons currently found in reserves in eastern Poland are in fact constructs, the products of zoo "experiments" to breed animals backward, selecting for primitive characteristics. The result is an animal that looks rather like the old tarpons probably looked before becoming extinct, but that is not the real thing at all. The so-called mustangs of the North American west are feral horses, descendants of domestic horses that have been allowed to return to a wild state. The Mongolian is all that is left, whatever names we may put on other horses. A studbook for the species has been maintained at the Prague Zoo.

There are several hundred Mongolian wild horses in zoos around the world, in close to a hundred zoos, and all were captive bred. There may be none left at all in Mongolia itself, for several reasons.

When first discovered (probably by Europeans in the 1870s, during an expedition financed by a Polish nobleman, Count Przewalski) the Mongolian wild horse ranged widely in the Gobi Desert on the boundary of Mongolia and China and into suitable habitat in both countries as well.

The herds moved along the southern slopes of the mountains in the region and into the valleys in autumn and winter and out onto the Gobi Desert in spring and summer. The species is dependent on water sources and, unlike many other desert animals, cannot go long without drinking. The horses are shy and easily driven away from water by nomad encampments and herds of livestock.

Several factors have contributed to the Mongolian wild horse's decline. First, its shynes. When driven away from water, particularly in an area where its sources are few, as well as away from suitable grazing, the horse will perish. It stops reproducing, or reproduces more slowly than normal, and foal mortality is high. The second factor is hunting. Stockmen, less than sentimental about an animal that competes with their stock for food and water, have hunted the wild horses. As rifles improved in long-range performance (and were equipped with telescopic sights), the nomads took a terrible toll. Driven from food and water, frightened away from suitable habitat, and shot at at every opportunity, the herds were bound to shrink.

There has been an additional insidious factor—hybridization. The Mongolian wild horse breeds readily with domestic horses, which are probably their own descendants from thousands of years ago, but are now a different species. Once hybridization occurs, it either produces "mules," animals that cannot themselves reproduce; or, if the young are fertile, the original species is eroded until it vanishes. When there are more domestic horses, either temporarily wild like the American mustang or simply let out to free range until collected again, than there are truly wild horses, the wild horse is consumed by the inevitability of genetics. There are not that many cases where domestic animals can hybridize wild species, but where it occurs it is probably the most cryptic assault that can be made on wildlife. The only possible "cure" would be to eliminate all domestic animals that could become a factor—i.e., breeders—which would be unacceptable. Even if it were done, no one could be certain that the damage had not already occurred and domestic genes implanted. It is not a matter of some hypothetical "purity" that is the cause for concern. Changes in behavior, stamina, who knows how many characteristics, are inevitable. A species widely hybridized is an extinct species.

Zoos can have as many Mongolian wild horses as they want. Herds are widely dispersed and the studbook is intact. Like an increasing number of species, the North American bison, the European wisent, the Père David's deer, all are now permanently under human management. Control has come to man not because it was desired but by default. There was no other way for the species to survive. Bison can be released back into the wild. Although they can breed with domestic cattle, the scenario where this would occur is difficult to conjure up (and the hybrids would be detectable) but where can the Mongolian wild horse go and not encounter its genetic foe, its own descendant, the domestic horse?

# Père David's Deer

## ELAPHURUS DAVIDIANUS

A serious zoo-policy controversy arises when a species is known to be extinct in the wild. That controversy is well illustrated by a statement made in 1962 by the late Fairfield Osborn, then president of the prestigious New York Zoological Society. Mr. Osborn wrote in the 1962 edition of the *International Zoo Yearbook* (volumne 4):

"Zoos have little or no right [sic] to exhibit forms of animals whose continued existence in the wild is highly doubtful, except for the fact that in certain cases zoos can play a highly important part in preserving species whose numbers are few in the wild state or who have actually disappeared."

Having directly contradicted himself once, Osborn proceeded to underscore the confusion:

"Striking captive propagation successes have been scored in the case of the Père David Deer ... the Wisent ... the Przewalski wild horse ... and the Nene. ..."

Indeed, is an animal that is extinct in the wild, but doing extremely well in zoos an endangered species? And, as Fairfield Osborn suggests they should and they shouldn't, should zoos exhibit them as wild animals? Osborn's answer is yes and no.

One of the examples Osborn offers is probably the best test case there is because of the time frame involved. This example is the Père David's deer *(Elaphurus davidianus),* the only member of its genus and situated on the even-toed hoofed animals' family tree somewhere between moose and reindeer on one side and Asia's sambar stag on the other. As far as we know, since the 1600s, there have been no Père David's deer at all in the wild in their native China, where the animal's original range is pure conjecture. The peripatetic French priest who brought the giant panda and any number of other natural wonders to the attention of western scientists found a herd of the peculiar and not very handsome deer in a game park, maintained on the emperor's palace grounds for his amusement. That was in the nineteenth century. The deer had been extinct as wild animals for well over two hundred years when science first learned of them. Was it then a wild animal, and is it one today?

In any one year, between forty and fifty zoos produce Père David's deer fawns. There are always over a thousand in captivity in well over a hundred collections. By zoo standards that is hardly a rare animal, although it does not exist in the wild and hasn't for nearly four hundred years. Yet it is not a domestic animal. It is suspended.

Some people are surprised to learn that domestic animals have been swept with a wave of extinction, too, and that a very large number of breeds are endangered today. As new breeds have been evolved by selective breeding, the ancestral breeds typically have been allowed to become extinct. The same is true of cultivated plants, which is all the more surprising since all that had to be done was seed banking.

If cattle were raised without handling, or with minimum manipulation, and allowed to establish their own social order without interference for several hundred years, they would be about where Père David's deer are, except they would have started out as a species whose genes had already been manipulated. Without controls, however, they would revert to a more primitive type if the criteria for a bull's breeding success were simply how rough and tough he was. When dogs are allowed to run wild they mate without regard for breed (all domestic dogs belong to the same species) and before too many generations pass they all begin to look like the prototype pariah dog that can be found around villages and markets all over Africa, Asia, and Latin America.

It is true, of course, that the Père David's deer started out as a wild animal, was driven somehow to near extinction, and some were saved for the emperor of China's personal pleasure, apparently just in time. Zoos picked up and, still classifying the deer as a wild animal, continued to breed and disperse, breed and disperse until it is all over the world in substantial numbers. But always in captivity.

It is the opinion of the authors that the species should be allowed to continue its zoo career, but with an eye to finding appropriate habitat in China for controlled releases. That is the only way zoos can really fulfill their mandate, by completing the task.

# Cyprus Wild Sheep

## OVIS ORIENTALIS OPHION

The wild sheep of the eastern Mediterranean were certainly among the most important wild animals in history, as far as man's economics and life-style are concerned. They are believed to have given rise to the domestic sheep of which man has selectively bred at least eight hundred breeds. There are probably 800 million domestic sheep now in flocks around the world. Domestication probably took place between ten and eleven thousand years ago. It is true that no wild sheep has the domestic sheep's wool coat but there is an undercoat grown by wild sheep that shows that the potential is there. Another clue is that when sheep return to the wild, become feral, and are no longer bred for specific characteristics, they begin to lose that heavy wool coat.

One candidate for all or part of the domestic sheep's ancestry is the variously named Cyprus wild sheep, Cyprus red sheep, or mouflon. Its scientific name is also a matter of controversy and it may properly be *Ovis orientalis ophion* or *Ovis nusimon* or *Ovis laristanica* or some other name yet. Mammalogists are still arguing about it. What matters, though, is that the animal is becoming increasingly rare. It has been hunted for food and sport and because it competes with domestic sheep for forage, although the domestic sheep wield the greater pressure. Domestic sheep, often grazed in very large flocks, are among the most unrelenting foes the wild sheep have had to face.

Ironically, man has been as careless with his domestic breeds as he has been with wildlife and a very large and ever growing number of domestic breeds are endangered just as their wild forebears are. Many breeds of sheep are on the Rare or Minor list published by the American Minor Breed Conservancy. Between the loss or endangerment of both wild species and domestic breeds of sheep and goats, cattle and horses, swine and fowl of all kinds, the available biological diversity on this planet is becoming very skimpy indeed.

About twenty zoos exhibit Cyprus red sheep (as it is known in the census done by the Zoological Society of London), with an estimated two hundred or so specimens. Interestingly enough, not very many are reported born although the game reserve in Israel near Carmel has had births. It is a priority species to the Nature Reserves Authority there who see it as a biblical animal of enormous influence in the region. A terrorist raid on the preserve near Carmel claimed the lives of many of the animals there and the fate of the reproducing Cyprus sheep flock is not known.

There has been so much political instability at the eastern end of the Mediterranean in the last few decades, it is impossible to judge the status of animals in the wild and certainly predicting their fate is out of the question. It is difficult to get people in a region torn by war, revolution, and terrorism to concentrate on wildlife that has no immediate economic or survival value to them. There is a terrible irony there and an awful truth. The world's wildlife has not only been subjected to senseless slaughter, and unlimited displays of greed and indifference, but it is also one more unwitting victim of human politics. That may be the most difficult enemy of all to survive.

The actual history of the domestication of animal species is highly speculative at best. We have some archaeological evidence, some cultural, some artistic, and not just a little ancient and modern mythology. There is every indication, though, that sheep did arise as domestic animals near the region where the Cyprus wild sheep was once found in large numbers. It would be a poor way to repay the debt by letting conditions deteriorate so far that this probable ancestral animal vanishes for all time. The zoos are quite probably the species' last hope—and for that matter, man's, too.

# Chinese Goral

## NEMORHAEDUS GORAL

Somewhere between the antelopes and the mountain goats on the mammalian family tree come two species of rather goatlike animals known as gorals. One of these, the common goral *(Nemorhaedus goral),* until recently ranged from Siberia southward through China to Burma and Thailand including the Himalayan region. These small animals, which can weigh as much as seventy pounds or so, prefer rugged, wooded mountain slopes up to an altitude of about twelve thousand feet. They seem to pick the roughest terrain possible often with very precipitous cliffs, which they negotiate without apparent difficulty. They live on twigs, shrubs, grass, and nuts, almost anything their remote habitat has to offer. They require a regular supply of water and are most active during the morning and evening. During the day, they lie motionless on exposed rocks and are quite difficult to spot. On overcast days, they may forage all through the daylight hours.

The gorals move around their mountain fastness in small groups, anywhere from four to a dozen animals, and communicate with hissing and sneezing sounds.

The gorals are not spectacular trophy animals but, perhaps because of the challenge of getting near one (and recovering it after it has been shot), they have been hunted. The northernmost of the two species is now listed as endangered although a population count would be just about impossible to construct. Many of the areas where it is still found are far too remote for any reliable data.

Gorals do well in captivity. Witness the old-timer in San Diego that lived beyond seventeen. At any one time, ten or more zoos have gorals on display with a census, usually, of between twenty-five and thirty-five specimens. Three or four zoos report births every year; however, there have never been enough specimens in captivity to plan on repopulating any part of the animals' original habitat. It has not been a species very high on the "must" list for most of the world's zoos.

The goral represents a typical world wildlife conservation problem. It has been overwhelmed by events and almost brushed aside by more spectacular problems and flashier species. Few people from outside their natural range have ever seen a wild goral and few ever will. It is not the typical wild animal that lions, elephants, tigers, and rhinoceros are. Few people could even identify one if they read its name or saw one in a zoo. It is a kind of nondescript almost-goat.

There is far more to it than that, however. The goral represents the second most precious thing this planet possesses: biological diversity. (The first, of course, is the ability to sustain life.) Between the vast complex of cattle, deer, and antelope and the true goats and sheep come a small number of rather remote animals, the saiga, the gorals, the serows, the mountain goat, chamois, takin, musk-ox, and tahr. With the exception of the moutain goat (not truly a goat at all) and the musk-ox, they are all but unknown animals to the general public. Still, they represent a diversity that has enabled the complex world of mammals to function and evolve. Whether they are ancestral to better-known forms or are dead-end offshoots is not clear, but it is critical that as much diversity as possible be preserved. There is no logic at all to our being deeply concerned for the welfare of the African elephant and the Siberian tiger if we are relatively indifferent to the fate of the two species of goral, one of which is clearly in trouble. Although such choices are seemingly forced upon us, it is not our right to choose which animals to save.

# Szechwan Takin

## BUDORCAS TAXICOLOR TIBETANA

Tucked somewhere in between the North American mountain goat, the Alpine chamois, and the musk-ox on one side of the mammalian family tree and the wild goats, ibex, and bighorn sheep on the other are a couple of subspecies of strange animals not really very closely related to any other surviving species. These are the takins. The Szechwan takin *(Budorcas taxicolor tibetana)*, as its name suggests, is a native of southwest China, the province of Szechwan north to the Kansu border and south very nearly to the Yangtze River. Another subspecies of this strange, remote animal is found in Nepal and Bhutan to the west.

There is no count of how many takins there still may be or, for that matter, how many there should be to constitute a safe, healthy population. Nor is the extent of their original range known. The Chinese regard their takin as a rare animal, and since only the Chinese have had access to much of the animal's supposed habitat, we can only rely on their estimation.

The takin prefers very rough, remote country, up to an altitude of thirteen or fourteen thousand feet, so they are able to keep their secrets well. They stay in or near thick growths of rhododendron and dwarf bamboo near the tree line and only during the harshest winter months move down into sheltered valleys. Spring finds them again on grassy slopes and plains not far from cover. Their trails are distinct through the heavy growth where they have moved between grazing areas and salt licks.

Strangely the complex Chinese pharmacopoeia does not contain the takin as it does most other animals. It is known, however, that takin have been hunted for food and apparently make good eating for high-altitude people.

The takin does not live in areas where it is likely to be stumbled upon by the casual passerby. Anyone who has ever seen takins, much less studied them, had precisely that as an objective. The traffic is not great up where the takin, giant panda, and golden monkey dwell. There is evidence that the Chinese protect the takin, and human population pressure is not great in those high, remote areas. There has been some deforestation lower down the mountains, which could affect the takin's winter range but the impact has not been great. It should remain safe unless some unforeseen natural calamity occurs.

There are very few Szechwan takin in the world's zoo inventory. At any one time, there may be ten or so listed in the entire world. The zoos in East Berlin, San Diego, and Beijing have had captive births but the subspecies is not listed—Nepal/Bhutan or Szechwan. At present the zoos are not in a position to do very much if the news of the species in the wild should turn bad. They need more animals in widely dispersed collections with greater genetic diversity and more experience with the breeding species to have a backup population. This photo of a takin with young in the San Diego Zoo is a true rarity.

The takin presents a special problem faced by the world's zoos. Since it is not definite that the Szechwan takin is in jeopardy in the wild, is there justification or taking specimens for captive collections if they represent a rare but not officially threatened species? On the other hand, if we don't act now, zoos won't be able to help if the status of the animal changes or is found not to be as secure as previously thought. With the California condor, the zoos were forced to wait until it was almost too late. At the eleventh hour, they had to take all of the condors alive into protective custody. They had no choice—only a few birds were left and no young had been reported. With the nene, or Hawaiian goose, it was much the same thing. It is a kind of damned-if-you-do, damned-if-you-don't situation. Zoos have neither the space nor the budget to take in a survival nucleus of everything, and the choices are often tough. It is a risky situation either way.

# Philippine Tarsier

## TARSIUS SYRICHTA

The Philippine tarsier *(Tarsius syrichta)* has been found on several of the Philippine islands: Mindanao, Bohol, Siargao, Dinagat, Samar, and Leyte. Undoubtedly it has occurred on some of the seemingly endless number of smaller islands in between the larger strongholds as well. The full extent of the species' original range will never be established. Fossil remains of animals so delicate in structure, so small in bulk are always disappointing. A full-grown tarsier will weigh no more than six ounces. Unless there were once giant forms, we will find it difficult to reconstruct either its ancient history or its modern.

The gestation for the species is less than a month, and one young is born. That baby, however, is precocious. It is well furred at birth, its eyes are open, and it is able to both climb and hop on a level surface. It has to be a month old or so before it is able to execute the prodigious leaps that keep the adults one step ahead of trouble. At birth that infant weighs less than an ounce. Precocious young are not a hallmark of the primates, and this form is quite primitive.

The United States Department of Agriculture lists the Philippine tarsier as *threatened* while the International Union for the Conservation of Nature lists the species as *endangered*, its highest level of concern. Somewhere in between, perhaps, lies the awful truth. Like the other two (or possibly three) tarsier species, this fragile little animal may face the end of its history in our time. There have been terrible wars and great political unrest leading to military action in this tarsier's range over the last century. Wars aren't any better for wildlife than they are for people. There has been an unencumbered timber industry that has cut trees down without any concern for wildlife's needs. There has been deforestation for charcoal production and for ground clearing for highly questionable agricultural schemes. Much of the tarsier's habitat has been preempted and much of it simply destroyed.

Under the best of circumstances the Philippines would not be the best place to be an animal, any animal. To be a member of a species with no apparent use as food or other economic imperative is to be practically nonexistent. It would be difficult to explain to a resident of Leyte, or one of the lesser islands in the Philippine tarsier's range, the necessity of maintaining biological and genetic diversity. It is hard enough to get the message across among college-educated politicians in the developed nations of the West.

There are very few Philippine tarsiers in captivity, and they have been bred but not in important numbers. Duke University's Primate Center has them and so do one or two zoos, but there is nothing even resembling a captive population reserve should the wild population crash. There is no way of telling how many tarsiers constitute a safe wild population or what the survival dynamics may be. Females of most, if not all, vertebrate species can be very choosy and pick males according to the splendor of their display. If there are too few males, a female may just stop breeding. No one knows what might constitute too few males.

The day the last Philippine tarsier dies in some remote forest spot on some lesser island in that vast archipelago will not be recorded in any history book. There will be no mourning because the event will not be recognized or heralded. It may in fact not be until dozens of years have passed that concerned scientists will finally agree that the event must have taken place in the past. A little head shaking is about all that will mark the memory of this ancient primate that followed its own evolutionary course for so many millions of years, its numbers forever uncounted. Perhaps some genetic testimony to the species' existence will still exist in zoos and scientific collections like that at Duke, but unless there is some major breakthrough, there will probably never be enough Philippine tarsiers to release back into the wild on some island that has remained intact. The fragile existence of the Philippine tarsier sounds very much like the "twice-told tale." It is a leitmotif of our times.

# White-Handed Gibbon
## HYLOBATES LAR

The gibbons and siamangs, now recognized as being in their own family, Hylobatidae, are known as the *lesser apes.* Besides the gorillas, chimpanzees, and orangutans, they are the only apes that have survived into modern times. One of the gibbons, the lar, or white-handed gibbon, is found in a variety of colors: black, brown, buff, and cream. The hands and feet are always white. Their range has included southern Burma, Malaya, Thailand, Cambodia, Sumatra, and a number of adjacent islands where they may or may not still survive.

The very large range that the white-handed gibbon has occupied would seem to suggest large numbers, but predictably that is not the case. It has been estimated that there are no more than 250,000 left in that huge area of southern Asia. Agriculture and logging have pressed the animals into ever smaller pockets, cutting them off from each other and leaving them exposed to the hazards that are a natural result of a burgeoning human population. The animals are shot, trapped, and sold into the pet trade. Mothers are killed to get the infants they are carrying, most of which die anyway. Family life is disrupted and the dispersion of genetic material is blocked by isolation.

Gibbons are almost exclusively arboreal. They swing hand-over-hand through the trees at incredible speeds and with stunning agility. They do not like to travel on the ground and will not do so for long distances. If trees are cut and areas cleared, then, the animals are trapped. One estimate predicts that at the present rate of logging and land clearing for agriculture between 80 and 90 percent of the gibbons left, including the lar and excepting only a few species, could be gone in less than twenty-five years. It doesn't seem possible that man would be willing, for any reason, to allow his closest kin, the apes, to vanish but that is the case with the chimpanzee and gorilla in Africa, the orangutan and the gibbons and siamangs in Asia. We could very well lose them from the wild.

Between forty and fifty white-handed gibbons are born in the world's zoos every year, but that number could not come close to repopulating anything but a very small colony if an area could be thoroughly secured. It would probably be best if an uninhabited island could be purchased or donated to this cause and if it was within the ape's natural range.

The overall zoo population of the white-handed gibbon is substantial, so common are they that the species is not even registered under the rare animal zoo census by the London Zoological Society that publishes zoo statistics.

The white-handed gibbon is apparently more adjustable than most of the other apes. In the wild, it inhabits all types of forests, keeping from sixty to almost two hundred feet above the ground. It is found in hillside evergreens, both dry and moist deciduous growth, dry evergreen and tropical rain forests. About a quarter of its waking time is spent eating, virtually always aloft, feeding on fruit for the most part, but some leaves, buds, and tender branches and some insects. It can run with startling agility along the heavier tree limbs, balancing itself with its enormously long arms. It spends most of its time, however, on the more slender branches where it is less likely to fall prey to a marauding cat. It occupies what is known as the "small-branch niche" in the tropical forest community.

There is neither logic nor ethics in expressing concern for one plant or animal that is threatened or endangered over another in that condition. In the truest sense, any species is of inestimable value as part of this planet's precious biological diversity. A pupfish in Death Valley, a small marsh plant in New England, grand landmark species with tremendous public relations value such as the Siberian tiger or the whooping crane, a mole in California, or a gibbon in Asia—it all amounts to the same thing. Their likes shall not be seen again on this planet and in all likelihood anywhere in the cosmos where hopefully one day life almost certainly will have taken a different turn. Still, the apes provide us with a sense of kinship, they are our unmistakable link to the animal kingdom not because *they* are our ancestors, which they are not, but because we both come from very ancient but common stock. Intellectually and emotionally we are closer to the apes than to the pupfish, although that is not really a very productive, scientific way of evaluating things. Still, the loss of an ape seems a major crime against our planet and all life. It may be happening on a broad scale far sooner than we dare believe.

# Siamang

## HYLOBATES SYNDACTYLUS

The siamang *(Hylobates syndactylus)* is another of the lesser apes. It is in the same genus as the gibbons but represents by far the largest species in the grouping. Siamangs have a five-foot armspread. For an animal that usually weighs no more than twenty-five to thirty pounds, that is enormous. It gives these apes unbelievable agility aloft, where they spend most of their time.

On the ground or on a good exposed branch, the siamang runs very fast, waving its long slender arms to achieve perfect balance. Should one slip or fall, there is virtually no chance it will go far before it has a hold on a branch and is swinging up and over it in great gyrating pinwheel movements. The siamangs are among the most agile of animals.

The siamangs have a smaller range than some of their co-genitors. The species has been limited in historical times to the mainland of Malaysia and the island of Sumatra. There are distinctions between it and the other gibbons. The siamang has webbing between the second and third toes. What most singles it out is its incredible voice and vocalizations. It has a throat pouch that inflates when the animals, in the wild and in captivity as well, join in a group singsong that must be heard to be believed. In the wild, these singsongs serve several real purposes. They help the troop stay in touch in dense forest growth, and they clearly define territory. They may even intimidate enemies. But in captivity a songfest is a social happening. I don't think it is projecting to say the animals enjoy these social hollering and bellowing sessions. Zoo professionals with a siamang troop in their care can generally trigger the awesome torrent of sound by giving a whooping signal. The animals pick it up and, pumping and inflating their air sacs, may keep it going for as long as ten to fifteen minutes. No one who witnesses this phenomenon is likely to foget it.

What, if any, individual communications arise from these sessions is not known. It is likely the singsong serves three purposes: keeping in touch, declaring territory, and providing the unifying feeling that comes from a community sing. It is not unlike our use of folk songs and old familiar melodies around the campfire and at least one aspect of hymns and Christmas carols. Making noise together—musical by our terms or not—brings people together and apes, too. Many of the apes generally, particularly chimpanzees and these lesser apes, appear to love being noisy. It doesn't take much of an excuse to set them off. What that does or does not have to do with the beginnings of language is not yet known.

The captive population of siamangs is substantial, with thirty or more born in zoos in a good year. They should have space and in the proper climate, or at least at the right time of the year, they should have outside areas with elaborate gymnastic bars and poles set well above the ground and isolated by a wide moat. The moat can be shallow but it should be wide. With their shouting sessions, sounds that can be heard at the far ends of even the largest zoos, and their aerial acrobatics that can only be described as awesome, siamangs are extraordinarily attractive zoo specimens. They do bring people in and they are needed as a breeding reserve. They now breed well enough so that any zoo that has the budget to provide sufficient indoor and outdoor display space can build its colony from captive-bred animals. There need not be nor should there be any further impact on wild populations that have more than enough to contend with from deforestation for the timber industry and clearing for agriculture.

Siamangs are being seriously threatened by apparently limitless human population growth. The apes just might not survive us, especially if we deprive them of their essential forests. The siamangs evolved to live in trees and that is where they must be to live and feed and breed.

# Snow Leopard

### PANTHERA UNCIA

One of the most beautiful cats in the world is also one of the least known. The magnificent snow leopard *(Panthera uncia)* had a much larger range even a century ago than it does now, but that range can't be defined for sure. The snow leopard is a high-altitude cat that only descends into wooded valleys in the dead of winter. It prefers to hunt its rapidly vanishing prey between the tree line and the permanent snow line. It can't really survive for long in wooded areas.

At one time the 150-pound snow leopard probably ranged from northern Iran into Turkmenistan and from there north and east into regions of the USSR, China, and Mongolia. The extreme southern range was probably northern India. Today it is pretty well limited to the high mountains of Central Asia and southern Siberia, which include the Tibetan Plateau and western Szechwan. It can also still be found in Pakistan and Afghanistan.

That a cat of such remote regions should be all but done in by man is astonishing, but that is clearly the case. Deforestation of its winter valley retreats probably had little to do with its demise. Its prey was killed, shot out from under it, and it often had to turn to livestock. The mere presence of a large predator is a challenge to the mountain people, who are just about always armed. When that predator takes livestock, the challenge turns into a compulsion; so this cat has been hunted relentlessly.

For years it was the ultimate recreational kill for trophy hunters, but very few had the stamina to stalk so elusive a quarry for weeks at a time at high altitudes. Trophy hunting by outsiders, who did not belong to the world above the tree line, did not figure very heavily in the snow leopard's woes. It was a factor, but the least of several.

The most pressing factor has undoubtedly been the cat's unbelievably beautiful coat. From Pakistan, China, the Soviet Union, and everywhere the cat ranged as well as from areas well beyond their range, the skins appeared in the fur markets. Traders traveled endlessly and encouraged stockmen and professional hunters among the native peoples, who had the best opportunities to encounter the cats, to kill as many as possible. The skin of the snow leopard has always been one of the highest-priced in the world.

The snow leopard is now at least nominally protected over nearly all of its remaining habitat, and most nations will no longer permit the export or import of their hides. Some still get through, of course, but the traffic is dying down. The last countries to ban them will be in Asia, but that ban will come. Because the animals are so remote today, hopefully there will be some left to breed.

Although the skin trade was probably the single biggest factor in the snow leopard's decline, it will be ultimately easier to deal with than the traditional treatment of all animals, particularly predators, by mountain people. They, too, live remote lives and are not very troubled by the opinions (or the laws) of outside people. Like the leopards they kill, they know well in advance when they are being approached by strangers. And like the leopard, they can dissolve into a landscape of rivers and mountain passes that has been only roughly mapped. Certainly the hidden caves and ravines appear on no charts. Like the cats they kill, they can tolerate the altitudes and extreme weather conditions as no outsider can. The mountain people and the leopard share a hidden and forbidding world.

A studbook for captive snow leopards is maintained at the zoo in Helsinki, Finland, and a great many cats have been bred in captivity—in some zoos, generation after generation. Since a snow leopard born to a captive mother almost certainly could not be put into the wild, the zoos are not the ideal solution for saving the species. However, if it comes to that, at least the zoos are in a position to do their share. They have the cats, they have the genetic records, and they have the curatorial experience. With captive breeding records as good as they are and with the likelihood that at least some of the cats will survive in the wild once the traffic in their hides is ended, it seems likely that endangered though the species may be, we will not enter the next century without them. The loss of anything as magnificent as the snow leopard would be intolerable.

# Siberian Tiger

## PANTHERA TIGRIS ALTAICA

Of all the great cats left on earth none surpasses the great Siberian, Manchurian, or Amur tiger (all names for the same cat, subspecies *Panthera tigris altaica*) in size or, in the estimation of most people, beauty. A large specimen can measure thirteen feet in length (tail included) and, in the wild, weigh up to seven hundred pounds. Captive specimens tend to put on more weight from a steady supply of meat, requiring no effort on their part to obtain.

Originally these giant hunters were found across Siberia, in Northern China and Manchuria, and south into Korea. It is thought their fossil remains rest uncovered in Japan as well. Since the Siberian tiger's range probably came close to overlapping that of the subspecies we call the Chinese tiger *(C. t. amoyensis)* and possibly the ranges of extinct cats we would recognize as other subspecies if they had survived into our time, its exact range will never be known. Although some races or perhaps just individuals did in fact roam above the Arctic Circle, finding a comprehensive fossil record at high altitudes in Arctic conditions is neither easy nor reliable.

Like all tigers, the giant Siberian is a hunter and eats virtually nothing but meat. In the far north, it hunts any hoofed animal whose range it encounters. At high altitudes, it takes wild goats and sheep and even hunts the large and potentially very dangerous Asian brown bear, an animal that may be twice the tiger's weight. Where natural prey is scarce, it will kill livestock, and that, plus the market value of its hide, has made it a target for native hunters. In India, Hong Kong, China, and a good many other Asian markets as well, even a small Siberian tiger skin poorly preserved will bring from $3,000 to $5,000. The animal has always been considered a major big-game trophy, one of the most difficult to hunt.

The total number of Siberian tigers remaining in the wild is not known, but most estimates place it well under two thousand. There are more in captivity than in the wild today, and that is likely to remain the case as far into the future as we can project. The animals breed extremely well in captivity—too well, in fact—and it should be possible to maintain a diverse captive breeding population. There are two major problems.

Less responsible zoos and private wild-felid collections continue to breed indiscriminately without reference to the studbook that has been maintained for years at the Leipzig Zoo in East Germany (where the animal is inevitably referred to as the Amur tiger) or to the International Species Inventory System, a computerized breeding advisory directory at the Minnesota Zoological Garden near Minneapolis. Inbred cats without a reliable pedigree could eventually wipe out the species. Responsible collections today do not cross the Siberian with the other seven tiger subspecies (Chinese, Caspian, Javan, Bengal, Sumatran, Indochinese, and Bali) and certainly not with other big cats like lions; nor will they breed even pure Siberian tigers to each other without reference to multigenerational breeding records. There is no longer any excuse to risk the diversity without which a species loses vitality and, eventually, its identity, nor is there any justification for hybrids. Hybridization, even involving subspecies, is just creeping extinction.

The second problem is less easily solved. As wild ranges are encroached upon more and more by man, and as natural game vanishes, there will be ever fewer places where the giants, with their large food demands, can live. Worse yet, no one knows how to return a captive-born Siberian tiger to the wild. It learns to hunt from its mother, and if the cat is the descendant of generations of captive animals, as is the case with the vast majority of Siberian tigers being held today, hunting for their own survival may not be even remotely possible. Since tigers are rigidly solitary in their ways, they do not take up with other cats, as some lions might, and subsist with and learn from a pride. That is difficult enough to do with lions, as the late George Adamson learned, and of course lions are native to regions where prides and hunting associations are the cat's way of life and where game is dense and dependable. Near the Arctic circle or high on ice fields in remote Asian mountain ranges, it is probably impossible. So the Siberian tiger seems almost certain to be one of those species for which captivity is the only choice. This is not to suggest that more cats should be removed from the wild, except, perhaps, to gain new vitality in the captive gene pool. The records today are good enough and the cats widely enough dispersed in collections around the world to permit the species to continue far into the future. Yet captive Siberian tigers may have to be captive forever.

# Snow Monkey
## MACACA FUSCATA

The Old World monkeys—the monkeys of Africa and south and east Asia—belong to the family Cercopithecidae. There are an estimated eighty-five species over that vast range and they occupy a variety of niches, whatever their varying habitats have to offer. The macaques, genus *Macaca*, is one of the largest groups, with at least nineteen species. They range from Borneo and Thailand to Afghanistan, India, Taiwan, Japan, northwestern Africa (the Barbary ape discussed elsewhere in this book), Nepal, and China. It is a huge range for a single genus.

The Japanese macaque *(Macaca fuscata)* is one of the strangest of the lot, for it is the animal known by the unlikely name of snow monkey. When we think of moneys, we naturally think of steamy climates, which is not exactly accurate. Many monkeys in Africa live where the temperature can go down into the fifties at night, and even below at some altitudes. But the Japanese macaque had a very special adaptation to make.

The islands where the macaque is found in Japan are the big island of Honshu, as well as Shikoku, Kyushu, and Yakushima. When the macaques made it to the Japanese archipelago long ago, they found islands and altitudes that experienced significant snowfall during a part of the year. The rhesus monkey *(M. mulatta)* found the same thing in Afghanistan. But snow creates a problem. Female macaques nurse their young for about a year, and then their milk stops flowing. In times of heavy snowfall, food can become scarce and infant mortality too high for the species to sustain and still survive. The snow monkey's special adaptation is a continued or possibly a stop/start lactation. Well after the weaning age, young can still return to their mothers and nurse when food becomes difficult for inexperienced animals to find. It is undoubtedly this special adaptation that has enabled the well-furred Japanese macaque to survive where other monkeys might well have failed. In captivity, even when the weather is really harsh with freezing sleet and snow, Japanese macaques, given a choice of being indoors or out, will frequently huddle together against the weather in their display area until they are virtually encased in ice and snow. To the uninitiated zoo visitor it can look like cruel and unusual punishment. It is not. The macaques simply feel at home, which is about the nicest thing you can do for a zoo animal.

At what stage the alteration in normal macaque lactation pattern developed and how the monkeys fared before it was in place cannot be ascertained for certain. Long ago, the gregarious, tough, flexible ancestral monkeys of this widespread genus somehow reached Japan, which was a fair distance offshore from the Asiatic mainland, and there evolved into a separate species as macaques had been doing all over Asia and, to a very limited extent, in northernmost Africa. Once thoroughly evolved from that ancestral form, they adjusted to a potentially harsh winter climate and perhaps it was as this was happening that they spread their range into higher altitudes and more exposed habitats. And thus the snow monkey came into being.

Since the population reports of 1923, the numbers of Japanese macaques have been declining in large part because of deforestation, that ugly recurrent theme of much of wildlife's woes over most of the world. The macaques are protected in Japan, which is to say, they are not destroyed directly—nobody hunts them. But the destruction of their tree habitat is even more deadly. A monkey with trees to retreat to can hide from a man with a gun, but where does a monkey go when the man is armed with a chain saw?

There are a great many Japanese macaques in zoological collections and the number of captive births each year is well over a hundred. With careful attention to genetics, the species can be bred up and kept at about any level that meets the display demands of public institutions. Because they are gregarious and establish nicely defined social groupings, and because they don't have to be hustled inside when the temperature drops, like so many hothouse flowers, they make interesting animals to put on show. At the same time a strong reservoir of these animals remains on tap should it ever be decided to repopulate areas in Japan where the macaque has been seriously reduced or extirpated. They are also available should there be any further decline in the populations found there now. It is unlikely that the Japanese macaque will become extinct, although the population levels in Japan are nowhere near where they should be. The zoo-bred animals are a necessary backup against an uncertain future.

# Golden Monkey

## RHINOPITHECUS ROXELLANAE

The golden monkey *(Rhinopithecus roxellanae)* has also been known in its time as the snub-nosed langur. Because of its range and habitat, it has rarely been observed by scientists in the field since the explorer-priest Père David brought out the first skins in the 1860s. Much of its range of western China and possibly into remote parts of Tibet is under a thick blanket of snow for more than half the year. Its habitat is mountain slopes from sea level to ten thousand feet, often in thick rhododendron and bamboo jungles and coniferous forests.

Not only is the golden monkey seldom seen, it is assuredly a very rare animal. This splendid specimen in the Cincinnati Zoo is one of the few in captivity. A pair loaned to the zoo in 1988 by Chinese authorities was allowed to stay in Cincinnati for three months. A few golden monkeys are in zoos in China, notably in Beijing and in Chengdu, the provincial capital of Szechwan. The species is reported to have bred in captivity in one of those zoos. The Chinese, in fact, may be holding others in captivity, too.

The golden monkey shares the range of the giant panda: rugged forested slopes, freezing cold for much of the year and extremely difficult for humans to reach. The high, forbidding terrain among the clouds is inhabited by few people. Slightly farther down the slopes there has been some logging activity, but the Chinese have promised to have it stopped, lest it affect the range of the panda, the only animal they prize even more highly than they do this monkey.

When the species was named in 1870, it was probably already well on its way to being rare. Manchu officials once wore its fur as a badge of high station. The fur was always cherished, and the animals once heavily hunted, and the fur exported. The species has now been protected for decades by the Chinese authorities who look upon any interference with this animal as they would upon interferences with their panda—probably with lethal distaste.

The golden monkey travels through the trees in large troops, probably larger than the troops of any other arboreal primates. The monkeys are territorial and very noisy, wailing a strange human infant–like call through their noses. Unfortunately, as these troops are seldom encountered, their number, size, and location are not known. The troops come to ground for water and descend to lower cultivated valleys in the worst of winter. Otherwise they stay high in the trees, often starting small snow showers as they move from one snow-covered branch to another.

As things now stand, few people will ever see this remarkable-looking animal in the wild. It costs a small fortune to mount an expedition to get near where these animals might be found. Once there, there is no guarantee the local troop, if there is one, hasn't moved over into another valley.

If people cannot realistically expect to see even one of these monkeys, why be concerned for their existence? The answer really isn't very difficult, and it is echoed time and again in this book. The golden monkey represents part of this planet's extraordinary biological diversity. Scientists, Chinese as well as Western, can get to them if they need to. However many are left, the monkeys are where they belong, where they have a life-style peculiar to them and to no other species. They evolved to live in a strange, remote habitat. They share the weather and harshness with that other rare and cherished species, the giant panda.

As for seeing golden monkeys in zoos in any numbers, we probably will not. The Chinese government uses them as they use their pandas, as diplomatic pawns. It is a mark of special favor to be able to exhibit specimens even for a short period of time. In all of the world's zoos outside of China there are no more than twelve giant pandas. It is likely to remain the same with the golden monkey. One has to be satisfied to know that they are there where they came into being in their present form. One has to hope they always will be there in a kind of natural holding pattern. There is no way of knowing if that will be the case even a decade or two from now. Both the Chinese authorities and the golden monkeys are keeping their secrets well.

# Giant Panda

## AILUROPODA MELANOLEUCA

The giant panda is probably the best-known and most-beloved wild mammal species on earth. Almost any zoo that could raise the funds would pay the requisite million dollars for a pair, or perhaps purchase even one, knowing what a panda display would do for the zoo's gate. The Chinese know this well, and since they are the only possible source for pandas, they have used the animal as a (very expensive) export to make friends and influence people. The panda is probably the only wild animal functioning today as an authentic diplomatic tool.

No one knows what the giant panda's prehistoric range might have been, but almost all specimens in the wild today survive in western Szechwan Province. Pandas are somewhat limited by their food requirements and by their preference for altitudes above nine thousand feet. Although they are in the order Carnivora, they eat very little meat and live mostly on a few species of bamboo. The worse the weather, the better they seem to like it. Don't be deceived by the soft, cuddly look of a panda's fur. It is a formidable protective coat, as rich with lanolin as raw sheep wool, and very thick and coarse to the touch.

Not only is the original range of this mysterious animal unknown, but so is its actual *and* natural population. There are probably fewer than a thousand left in the wild, yet no one knows if that is as many as there are supposed to be or if it is only a fraction of a healthy population. Equally uncertain is their position on the mammalian family tree. Their species, *Ailuropoda melanoleuca*, is listed in the order Carnivora, but after that there is confusion. Some scientists put them in the family Procyonidae with the raccoons, kinkajou, and coatimundi, while others put them with the bears in family Ursidae. More and more, however, the idea is gaining currency that they should be a family of their own. Of course there are disagreements among mammologists (as there usually are) as to what that family should be called, Ailuropodidae or Ailuridae. Meanwhile, the giant panda, beloved by all, lives on benignly, perhaps a threatened or endangered species, or perhaps not.

Pandas do well as residents in zoos, but outside of China they have produced surviving young only in Madrid and Mexico City. The National Zoo in Washington, D.C., has made heroic efforts, but their female Ling-Ling has yet to have one of her young survive more than a few days, after three pregnancies. It has been discouraging and expensive. Still, tourists to Washington virtually always have the Smithsonian's pandas high on their must-see list. Millions of people have made the pilgrimage.

Since there is no certainty of the giant panda's present population or distribution, and since the part of Szechwan where they flourish is wild and remote, it is hard if not impossible to predict what role the zoos of the world will play in the species' survival. At any one time, there are usually only about a dozen specimens outside of China, and the manipulative Chinese government apparently intends to continue using its panda reserve as diplomatic pawns.

Yet it is unlikely that the great black-and-white bearlike animals will lose their place at the top of the wildlife popularity chart, and zoos around the world will continue to vie for China's largess. Seeing one in the wild is an extremely difficult task (this author has done it), and a very expensive one. So the few foreign zoos smiled upon by China's Foreign Office will offer the people of the world their only chance (unless they visit zoos in the People's Republic) to see alive and munching on bamboo the one animal everyone loves.

# Red Panda

## AILURUS MELANOLEUCA

Just exactly where the lesser or red panda *(Ailurus melanoleuca)* fits into the animal kingdom on the mammal's family tree is not clear. The arguments have gone on for years. "Definitive" texts differ even as to the animal's name. One gives it as *melanoleuca* and the next as *fulgens,* and they are talking about the same animals, a small, partially arboreal carnivore from Nepal, Sikkim, at least northern Burma, and two provinces in south-central China—Yunnan and Szechwan.

Traditionally the giant panda and the little red panda have been placed side-by-side somewhere between the bears and the raccoons with a great deal of discussion as to which way they lean. Recent studies have tended to break them up and put the little red animal in with the raccoons and kin (family Procyonidae) and the far better known giant panda in with the bears (family Ursidae). All that could change again at any moment.

What sets these two animals apart from both the raccoons and the bears is that they and they alone have developed a means of compensating for having no opposable thumb. They are flat-footed, but do have a wrist bone that can be rotated against the foot to form a kind of fist or grasping device. It is much more pronounced in the giant panda, where there is a real spur, but the red panda is the only animal known now or in the past with anything remotely analogous.

The red panda weighs about ten pounds and has a long, soft coat. The tail can be very nearly as long as the body. These animals inhabit mountain forests and thick stands of bamboo. By day they sleep in trees and they are active at dusk and dawn as well as all night. They are excellent climbers and apparently use trees for safe retreat and feed mostly on the ground. Their diet is made up of bamboo shoots, grasses, roots, fruits, and acorns. True to their carnivorous heritage they will also eat insects, eggs of all kinds, young birds, and small rodents. These are not solitary animals but generally travel in pairs or small family groups. They are by nature shy and gentle and have long been favorite animals in the international zoo trade.

The little panda is a common animal in zoos around the world and a dozen or more zoos a year report successful breedings and births. That is not a large number of animals, but the zoo population should now be self-sustaining as the young are dispersed to more and more collections and natural habitat exhibits are designed to encourage mating and cub-rearing. The wild stock should be left in peace, insofar as that is possible.

The wild population of lesser pandas simply cannot be reliably estimated. There are certainly many more of them than there are giant pandas, but beyond that, much about them must remain a mystery. They are generally not active during the day when they could be observed. They take to the trees when men are near, and they live very often in remote and inaccessible areas. It can take days of hard climbing and hiking under terrible conditions (they don't mind cold, wet weather at all) to get near their habitat even in densely populated China. In Szechwan, they are often reported up to nine and ten thousand feet in areas where the snow is three feet deep, and the slopes are wrapped in layers of clouds and mist.

Since there has been deforestation in some areas where it probably had good populations in the past, since it was formerly impacted by demands by zoos and museums, and since the animal's pelts have appeared on exotic fur markets in the Orient, we can assume the lesser panda has retreated to ever more remote areas in search of safety and peace. Since there were probably lesser pandas already there, they may have overpopulated some areas, while escaping from others where man was intruding. Forest clearing and agriculture have climbed the slopes and invaded the valleys that once belonged to rare animals—giant panda, lesser panda, and golden monkeys. We know the giant cousin of the little red panda and the golden monkey have been seriously affected, but less is known about this species. It would be safe and perhaps wisest to assume the worst and take all measures to increase captive breeding and protect wild stocks wherever they are still to be found. The likes of the little red panda is not going to evolve again on this planet. Indeed, we do not really know how this species came into being.

# Asian Elephant

ELEPHAS MAXIMUS

At one time the proboscideans ranged over vast areas of the earth's surface. In their final stages they were giants among the lesser animals that scurried about them in an almost unimaginable natural-history wonderland. Today all are gone but two, the African elephant *(Loxodonta africana)* and the Indian, or Asian *(Elephas maximus)*. The mammoths and the mastodons and all the rest are now found only in huge bone piles and in mountains of fossil tusks so vast that in Siberia they can be mined like a vein of ore.

We don't really know what happened to all of these giant species. That is a major problem because if we did fully understand what caused all those species to vanish, we might be able to head off the same fate that is apparently stalking the two species we have left. Weather, something we can do little about, certainly played a role and the coming of the recurring ice ages had to have been devastating. Droughts would have played their part, disease perhaps, and the possibility that some of the species were simply derelict. These would be species that were on a dead-end road, an evolutionary cul de sac, and time simply ran out on them.

But clearly, emerging, hunting man played a role as well. The proboscideans were always killed for skin and ivory. Without refrigeration, and with the hunters operating in small bands, the waste must have been enormous. Sites have been found where entire herds died at the foot of cliffs. The supposition is that early men and perhaps pre-men "hunted" the giants by starting strategically located brush fires to drive whole herds to their doom (the same technique was used on horses and bison). Fire would have driven even these giants of the earth on ahead, even over cliffs.

Although individual elephants (and this would have been true as well of their ancestral forms) have a relatively slow reproductive rate—usually a single birth after approximately twenty-one months gestation—they do reproduce rapidly within their herd structure. Because they are so extremely social, they apparently must have very large numbers to maintain a viable population with genetic diversity. They need large enough social structures so that males may come and go, sorting out among themselves which males are dom-

inant and may claim the available breedable females. The population dynamics of these animals may contain the seeds of their destruction. When populations fall below a certain level, the herds and then the species may self-destruct. This could describe the situation in which the remaining two species now find themselves. The wheel turns rather slowly for giant animals—unlike rodents or lagomorphs, fish or insects—and it is too soon for us to tell. We have really been interested in such problems for too short a time to have meaningful charts and graphs.

The Asian elephant does not usually carry the heavy tusks characteristic of the African species, so ivory poaching has been less of a problem. But many elephants have been removed from the wild for use as beasts of burden—a task at which they surpass all competition because of their enormous strength and their extraordinary intelligence. Normally native to India, Burma, Bangladesh, Nepal, Bhutan, Thailand, Cambodia, Laos, North and South Vietnam, Malaya, Borneo, Sumatra, and Sri Lanka, Asian elephant populations are now severely reduced everywhere and discontinuous. Deforestation and agriculture have cut the animals off into ever smaller pockets, many of which have suffered terribly from war and political instability. At best, the species can be described as vulnerable, and it seems unlikely, in fact, that it will last very far into the future.

There are an enormous number of Asian elephants in captivity. It is the species usually seen in zoos and circuses but very, very few are bred by these holdings. Many zoos exhibit only cows and don't even try for young. We are fortunate in having photographs of captive-born Asian and African elephants. That is pleasing, but not typical. Captive reproduction is such a rare occurrence considering the number of elephants being held that it cannot be looked upon as the eventual savior of the species, either species. Conservation in the wild, secured habitat, restricted access by people, except as tourists with cameras, will have to be the orders of the day or the world can expect to be without any of this ancient order of animals at all in the twenty-first century. It would be a terrible mark on man's scorecard as a planeteer.

# Asiatic Lion

## PANTHERA LEO PERSICA

Today, the lion *(Panthera leo)* is normally associated with Africa south of the Sahara. That has not always been the case. Reminding us of what we have lost, there still remains a tiny remnant population in northwest India, specifically in the Gir Forest Sanctuary in Gujerat State.

The Asiatic lion (the same species as the surviving African animals, but probably the subspecies *P. l. persica,* and almost certainly others as well) once ranged over much of India, the Middle East, North Africa, and Europe. Its complete range has yet to be defined, and may never be. Very likely many of the unforested areas of Europe, except those in the far north, were once included, for this is an open-land or savanna cat, not the "king of the jungle" of popular legend. Just a little more than a century ago, lions were still found as far east as Eastern India and as far west as Iran.

Lions in every area except south of the Sahara and in the Gir Forest have been hunted out of existence, both for sport and by stockmen in defense of their livelihood. With their natural prey of antelope and other hoofed animals being reduced in numbers by habitat loss, competition with livestock, and sport and food hunting, the great cats have had no choice but to turn to man's domestic animals. Conflict in such cases is inevitable worldwide, and where it occurs the predators always lose. That is the history of man and animals on earth.

Today the Asiatic lion is totally protected. Although population figures are often little more than guesses, there are probably somewhere between one and two hundred wild animals left in that one preserve in Gujerat. Protection, how-ever, is not an assurance of survival. Cultivators and stockmen regularly invade the lion's last preserve in India, and how many cats are killed and in what ways is simply not known except in the most fragmented reports. The stockmen have poison, traps, and guns at their disposal. The lion has only its wits. Those that are killed because they took a goat or a cow have no way of passing along that information as part of a genetic code. As a result, the lions continue to take prey of opportunity, and the people who often have no choice but to encroach on the lion's limited reserved lands continue to take vengeance.

There are probably as many Asiatic lions in captivity as in the wild. More than a hundred were reported in about twenty collections in recent years. A studbook on the species has been maintained at the Sakkarbag Zoo in Junagadh, Gujerat, but information is incomplete and there can be little doubt that some captive Asiatic lions have been crossed with African lions. And that is hybridization, the death knell for a species or subspecies.

The lion cannot hold out forever in India, even with its total protection on the books. And since there is no way effectively to reintroduce large predators whose parents did not hunt for survival, the Asiatic lion is almost certainly doomed to survive only as a captive animal. There appears to be no other way, what with India's human population continuing to grow and the demands for cultivatable land and livestock continuing to increase. We could pray for a different scenario, but the numbers would still contradict our fondest wishes.

# Bengal Tiger

## PANTHERA TIGRIS TIGRIS

The Bengal tiger *(Panthera tigris tigris)* is one of a probable total of eight subspecies of tiger. The others are the Caspian, Indochinese, Chinese, Siberian (or Amur), Sumatran, Javan, and Bali. Of the lot the Siberian or Amur tiger is by far the largest, the largest of all the world's cats, in fact. It can weigh as much as eight hundred pounds. The Bengal form comes in at about the middle rank, four to five hundred pounds.

The mighty Bengal once ranged from Pakistan (where it was probably extinct before 1910) to Burma. In all of that vast area including the entire Indian subcontinent, there probably are not many more than two thousand to 2,200 specimens left. When the British controlled India, the number of cats shot from elephant-back as "sport" was obscene. A dozen tigers would be shot in a single day. They were trapped, poisoned, and hunted, too, for the skin game. Tiger skins on the floor, on the wall, and in women's coats were in. Wealthy Indian rajas and visiting royalty rated little better as conservationists. Tigers were for killing, and no one seemed to question the ethics or conservation consequences of the mayhem.

There was also the bugaboo of protecting the human population against man-eaters. It is undeniably true that some tigers have turned to human beings as easy prey. Solving the problem, however, did not have to entail the mass destruction of one of the world's most magnificent forms of wildlife. It did and still does require the surgical removal of the usually lone cat causing the problem. In the Sunderban Islands of Bangladesh, at the top of the Bay of Bengal, the problem does seem to arise more often than in any other area where tigers are still to be found. There are experienced professional hunters, who are equipped to deal with the occasional man-eater, and using the one cat's predation as an excuse for mass extermination is an exercise in overextended nonsense. Trophy hunters who explained their recreational killing as necessary to save human lives were engaging in the same absurdity.

There is the problem, too, of livestock. Without question, individual tigers have taken to raiding cattle and domestic water buffalo, animals the people of India can ill afford to spare. No people, least of all rural people living very close to the poverty line, can be asked to suffer further hunger and deprivation because of an ethic that operates on some higher, holier plane. Again, though, the tiger is well enough known and there are professional hunters with more than enough skill (and ballistics) to surgically remove offending animals. Unless that is done wherever there is direct conflict with misbehaving predators, there is no chance any predators will survive much longer. With human population expansion on its present track, man and animal are going to have to live right up against each other over most of the world. Man, as presumably the more clever species, is the one to make the adjustments necessary. When work on the railroad through the Tsavo area of Kenya was halted because lions were killing workers just about every night, a single hunter, Colonel Patterson, tracked the two killers and removed them without bothering any other nonoffending lions, of which there were many in the area. Unless that same measure of concern for the tiger as a wild species is shown it could be eliminated within twenty to thirty years.

There are an enormous number of Bengal tigers in captivity. It is only in captivity that white tigers can be found. They are a relatively rare color variation of the usual yellow tiger. Like lions they reproduce readily, and cubs are generally a drug on the exotic animal market. It is difficult to find a zoo that needs them. Scores are born every year and are bred, in fact, in most cases because the cubs attract people, and zoos need people at the gate if they are to remain open. Tigers are sure breeders and sure attention getters. Our daily newspapers are forever showing tiger mothers with their cubs at the local zoo.

Captive-bred tigers, generations removed from the wild, can be finely bred using computerized genetic data, but the offspring are no more candidates for a return to the wild than any other predator that high up the scale. Tiger cubs learn to hunt—both what and how—from their mothers. If its mother doesn't know how to hunt, and there are no prey animals to practice on, the tiger is going to remain where it was born, in one zoo or another. It is a problem that has yet to be dealt with. If the tiger is to be a wild species as well as a zoo species, some major accommodations within their natural range are going to have to be made.

# Sika Deer

CERVUS NIPPON

Few forms of wildlife have had to interact with man as completely as the deer have. Man has taken them up and shipped them around the world as transplants used for sport, food, and decorations. And they have been, of course, hunted endlessly in their native habitats, again for food and sport and as decorations in the form of mounted trophies. Because they reproduce rapidly for large animals and because they are generally a resilient lot, they have faired better than most huntable species. In many areas, they are just about the only large wild animals to be found.

The sika deer *(Cervus nippon)* is found in a number of areas in North America and Europe including the British Isles, but that is the hand of man at work. The species (with it numerous subspecies) was originally found in Siberia, Manchuria, Korea, China, Vietnam, Japan, the Ryukyus Islands, and Taiwan. In many of those areas, the animal is now in trouble.

The Formosan sika *(C. n. taiouanus)* once abounded in the forests of the central mountain range of Taiwan, but it has been hunted to virtual extinction. These deer prefer dense high forests; so some managed to survive despite the relentless pressure. A few hundred deer have been farmed on Taiwan for their meat.

The Ryukyu or Kerama sika *(C. n. keramae)* is also endangered. It was almost certainly introduced from Japan early in the 1600s, but in those remote areas, it developed into a different animal. Goats were introduced to many of the same islands and did terrible damage to the habitat. Poor forage and uncertain water supplies in low rainfall years account for much of the deer's problems on these outposts in the Pacific.

The North China Sika *(C. n. mandarinus)* once had a large range in at least Shansi and Chihli Provinces, but excessive hunting pressure was more than the animals could take.

Some have been farmed for their meat (and antlers, which are considered medicine), but in the wild, trouble lies both behind and ahead. There is, or at least has been, a Shansi sika *(C. n. grassianus)* in China as well, but again overhunting, particularly for the deers' antlers, has brought them to the edge of extinction. In South China and in the Yangtze Valley, it has been the same story.

The sika in captivity does very well. It is an attractive animal to have on display with its reddish ground color and parallel lines of white spots. There is also an unspotted form. They are easy animals to manage and seem to reproduce under just about any conditions. It is one species that will reliably produce young to help attract crowds to the zoos. There are hundreds of specimens in the world's zoos, hundreds more on private land far from their original range.

There is an inevitable problem with captive breeding. Not all transplants and captive animals have necessarily come from the same subspecies. The scientifically managed collections, of course, have been as meticulous as they can be, but it is entirely possible that even some of their stock was adulterated along the way. We will never know for certain, but efforts are being made to weed out questionable specimens and reinforce those now held for breeding with known animals of certain origin.

The sika deer will not become extinct because of the large numbers transplanted and those held in zoological collections. What will happen to the wild stock is another question, and the answer is nowhere near as certain. Human population growth does result in the decimation of forested areas, livestock does compete for food and water, meat is needed in ever greater quantity, and, in the case of the sika deer, velvety antlers (when they first appear each year) are used in traditional medical remedies of highly questionable value. Man and deer are inextricably entwined.

# Wisent

## BISON BONASUS

The word bison (or incorrectly, *buffalo*) conjures up the image of massive herds thundering across the open plains of the American West. That is a true enough picture as far as it goes, but it is incomplete. The Old World bison, better known as the wisent *(Bison bonasus)*, is an animal of European forests. It looks a great deal like the American bison but is considerably less massive.

From prehistoric times well into historic times, the wisent ranged throughout western and southern Europe as far east as the Caucasus and northward at least to the Lena River in Siberia. By the early part of this century, they were nearly extinct everywhere. In 1925, the Caucasian race did in fact vanish and is now known to have become extinct. There are distinct parallels with the American bison, for they both nearly vanished altogether within a couple of decades of each other, and they both were brought back from small nuclei by the same kind of concern.

There are now three substantial herds in the forests of eastern Poland and between ten and twelve herds in the Soviet Union. The animals number in the thousands and are regulated just as they are in the United States and Canada. The so-called typical race of wisent is found in the only primeval forest left in all of Europe, Bialowiez in Poland, directly on the Soviet border. The area was a private hunting preserve for both Russian tsars and Polish kings. It survived devastation in World War II because Herman Goering had declared it his private shooting preserve and ordered the German troops to protect it. The small forest was used for executions and burial of prisoners but otherwise was left intact with its wisent, wild boar, and stag.

The wisent is bred regularly in dozens of zoos around the world. Both in captivity and in the wild, it is no longer threatened. The saga of this species and the parallel story of the American bison demonstrate that a species can be brought back from the edge of extinction. When enough people care enough, miracles can be worked. Both the American and the European bison herds were built up almost entirely from animals that were taken into protective custody and held until they were viewed in a new way by the people at large. To have left the few wild specimens of each species on their own less than a hundred years ago would have been to condemn them both.

If at any time in the future, the bison of North America or of eastern Europe should appear to be in danger again, the zoos can step in and rebuild populations. But it is far better to build and maintain herds working from as broad a base as possible.

Case studies like the plains bison of the New World and the wisent of the Old offer both encouragement and invaluable experience. The list of animals that have been snatched back from oblivion has been growing steadily and without doubt will continue to do so. Every story like that of the wisent inspires workers in the field of wildlife preservation, genetics, and reproductive physiology. Every species, of course, offers its own problems and what appear as similarities can make things seem deceptively simple. Herd-oriented hoofed stock, however, usually offer the easiest challenges. It will be quite different when the case to be dealt with is the mountain gorilla, where there is not a single specimen alive in captivity. Still, success is success and each such story reveals the one common ingredient that is essential for any species for which the attempt is made, determination.

# Gaur

## BOS GAURUS

The giant wild bovine we call the gaur *(Bos gaurus)* was found from peninsular India north to Nepal across Burma, Thailand, Laos, Cambodia, and Vietnam, and from there south along the Malayan peninsula in a number of subspecies. Typically found in hilly regions, it existed in large numbers. It preferred dense tropical forests with open glades and meadows where it could come out to feed at night. Days were spent back in the deepest part of the forest.

A combination of factors have conspired to reduce the world's wild gaur population sharply, and it is difficult to see how they can survive for long under present circumstances. One of the most devastating assaults has come from domestic cattle. Herds of sickly cattle have been regularly driven into prime gaur habitat and the wild giants (six feet or more at the shoulders) have contracted their diseases and been unable to fight off the infections. They died by the thousands. Some populations have been heavily impacted by war, being killed by everything from hungry troops to land mines and strafing attacks and bombing by aircraft.

Gaur were hunted for sport, for both meat and trophies, and have been driven away by all manner of land development schemes, water impoundments for agriculture, and by deforestation, which continues today.

The gaur is at least nominally protected in almost all areas where it still exists. But between deforestation and disease from domestic cattle who have little or no veterinary care, the outlook for the wild animals left is not good.

There is a studbook for captive gaur in the West Berlin Zoo and the captive breeding record is very encouraging. The animals have been bred from Brownsville (Texas), Oklahoma, Los Angeles, New York, San Diego, and St. Louis to Berlin and London, and that is not a complete list. At any one time there are generally well over a hundred gaur living in twenty or more zoos.

The species is a good subject for artificial insemination and embryo transfer, with dairy or beef cattle (ones that are disease free!) carrying the embryos as surrogate mothers. Using these modern and well-tested bovine reproductive techniques, the number of gaur in captivity could be built up to almost any level desired. With careful genetic control and regular dispersement of breeding nuclei around the world, and with breeding loans between zoos, the species can probably be kept going for as long as necessary.

If things ever do settle down in southeast Asia, gaur could be released back into the wild. Keeping subspecies going may be a bit more difficult because records may not be complete on some strains already breeding in captivity. Undoubtedly subspecies were mixed before careful record keeping was instituted. Since there is no longer any need to act with haste, greater care can be taken. Still, captive populations may never again be absolutely pure.

The gaur is a wild species that is so much like our domestic cattle that husbandry techniques common on modern farms can be applied to very good effect. Captive gaur can also be protected against bovine diseases using the same sera used on domestic cattle. So, while it may not look good for the wild gaur in the jungles of Asia, at least not in the long run, it does look very good for the buildup of captive herds and therefore, the salvation of this splendid species of wild bovine.

# Fallow Deer

## DAMA DAMA MESOPOTAMICA

The Mesopotamian fallow deer (variously given as *Cervus dama mesopotamica, Dama dama,* and *D. d. mesopotamica*) is a species that has, through the interference of man, become very well established in all kinds of places where it doesn't belong. At the same time it has become increasingly rare where it does belong—again because of human intervention.

There are introduced herds of this handsome little deer in Sweden, Russia, the United States, Canada, the West Indies, Argentina, Chile, Peru, Uruguay, South Africa, Madagascar, Japan, Australia, Tasmania, New Zealand, and Fiji as well as in the British Isles and other European locales. The shuffling began with this species with the Phoenicians and ancient Romans, who apparently introduced them to the European mainland. It is not clear if the Mesopotamian fallow deer is a separate species or a subspecies of the animal generically known as the fallow deer. At any rate, fallow deer were broadly dispersed.

While all this moving around was going on, the Mesopotamian form of the species was not faring at all well in its original range, which was the Mediterranean region of extreme southern Europe, Asia Minor, Palestine, Iran, and North Africa, including Ethiopia. There were deer of this or a similar species in Asia but the names of the Mesopotamian species and the Asian one have become too confused to know for certain what or which it was in truly ancient times.

Excessive hunting was a major threat and apparently climatic changes played their role. By the year A.D. 1000, it was gone from Ethiopia. It lasted in Africa until the nineteenth century but finally vanished, leaving not a single species of deer on the entire African continent, except, of course, for introduced herds of this species on Madagascar and in South Africa. By the early 1900s, the species was gone from the Greek mainland, and by 1950, it had been hunted out on Sardinia. The Asian population shrank to practically nothing, and of course the population in Morocco went with the rest of the African animals. In Iran and Palestine, the animal, apparently the Mesopotamian form, has been listed as endangered for years. In 1950, a very small herd was found along the border between Iran and Iraq but no one knows their fate since the recent deadly war that was fought there.

Considering how well the fallow deer adjusts to new habitats—from Sweden to Tasmania and the Fiji Islands—it is not surprising that there is a major breeding success story in zoos. Hundreds of fallow deer listed as *Dama dama* are born in zoos every year. Animals listed as *D. d. mesopotamica,* the Persian fallow deer, are bred as well but only a very, very few. Again, there may be some confusion over names and lineage.

What has happened to the so-called Persian fallow deer in Iran since the revolution can not be ascertained. Before the recent upheaval in the region, there were captive herds and preserves to protect the animals from the multiple threat of dams, hydroelectric projects, deforestation, and the assault of large numbers of domestic livestock on their habitat. How high the fallow deer has remained on the agenda of the Islamic revolution may not be known for years. The news may be very good, or it may be very bad indeed. It would be unwise to be overly optimistic.

The fallow deer will not become extinct simply because it has been moved around the world. The Mesopotamian form, whatever its proper taxonomic name may be, may not fare as well. Israel has gotten some animals and has been breeding them there. Unfortunately, they were mostly in the Carmel Hai-Bar preserve where recent terrorist attacks set much of the preserve habitat on fire. The results of that incident are also not yet fully revealed. The Mesopotamian form of the fallow deer has been much troubled by man. There doesn't seem to be any end to it, either. It is the species' misfortune to come from what is now probably the most politically troubled area on earth.

# Malayan Tapir

## TAPIRUS INDICUS

One of the most seriously endangered groups of animals left on earth is the order Perissodactyla, represented by the seventeen species of odd-toed ungulates. They have somehow managed, miraculously, to survive into our times. The order now includes only the eight members of the horse, zebra, and ass family (Equidae), four species of tapirs (Tapiridae), and five rhinoceroses (Rhinocerotidae). Once, during the ice ages and before, there were many, many more forms, but they are faint fossil memories now. The seventeen species left are under constant pressure and that condition does not show signs of abating.

Three of the four tapirs variously range from southern Mexico down to southern Brazil, while the fourth, the Malayan tapir *(Tapirus indicus),* is from Burma and Sumatra. Because the perissodactyls are ancient mammals and have such a poor rate of survival as species into modern times, there is always the danger that the small number remaining may die off. We cannot say it would happen without warning because we have been more than warned already.

Zoos have done their part to be sure that there is good captive stock of Malayan tapirs well dispersed around the world. War or deforestation in the tapirs' limited native range could spell doom. They are animals of forests, especially near rivers and other reliable water sources. They are hunted both by native peoples and by the big cats for food.

At any one time, there are usually between 125 and 150 Malayan tapirs in fifty to sixty zoo collections. Births are reported in fifteen to twenty zoos almost every year. A studbook for the species has been maintained officially at the San Diego Zoo since 1984 (the home of the specimens pictured here) and presumably contains records for every captive tapir in the world. It is now relatively simple to use the best husbandry techniques. Breeding loans and artificial insemination are among the tools of zoo directors, curators, keepers, and veterinarians.

What does it take to maintain even one tapir in captivity, keeping in mind that it comes from a tropical forest with an enormously complex selection of foodstuffs available to it?

Space, of course, and special diet. An animal as large as a large pony or small horse can't be kept in a cage, and tapirs are maintained in enclosures with as natural a look as possible. Weather extremes, such as draughts and sudden temperature drops, must be avoided because these animals are native to warm climates. If they are to breed and care for their young, they need privacy and some means of getting away from noisy crowds.

A diet for a Malayan tapir includes: grain, hay, vegetables, and a vitamin/mineral supplement. Milk and bread are also used by some zoos, and a few use raw eggs. Also dog chow, fish, and small birds as well as beef heart or some other muscle meat are used in some collections. The latter items are believed to replace the carrion that the tapir probably would utilize in the wild; it is not a hunting animal.

Most zoos cut the food they provide into "stewing" size and remove rough or tough stems. Greens are used cautiously because too many can cause stomach upset. The following foods are added routinely, but at different times and in varying quantities according to the age of the specimen and its physical condition: cooked rice, carrots, potatoes, and corn, soft fruits, bananas, curds, and yogurt. Tapirs in the wild eat natural laxatives, so rhubarb or some other plant-derived stool softener is recommended by veterinarians especially during transit or times of stress. Deaths in captivity with this species generally seem to have something to do with the softness and easy passage of their food.

These dietary requirements are listed in detail to show that keeping even one specimen of a highly specialized animal (and every species is, in fact, specialized) is an extraordinarily complicated and expensive proposition. If the forests where the Malayan tapir is at home are further impacted and the wild state becomes even less secure than it is now for all of the perissodactyls, the species can be saved, but at a cost and by very caring people with a high level of expertise. The captive Malayan tapirs of the world are now self-sustaining, but the zoos that are keeping them are obviously going to need proper support to do their work.

120

# Indian Rhinoceros

## RHINOCEROS UNICORNIS

The great Indian rhinoceros (that is its proper vernacular name; scientifically it is known as *Rhinoceros unicornis*) is an endangered species that once ranged over much of northern India and Nepal along the Himalayan foothills all the way to the border of Burma. It is not known how far to the south it was found.

This very ancient species must have tall grasses and reeds in wet areas, and small lakes with streams running between them. The deep grass helps the rhino cow keep its young safe from tigers that normally would share their range with them. All rhinos require muddy wallows to protect them from biting insects. Like most wildlife, its preferred habitat is very specific.

The great Indian rhinoceros bears a single horn on its nose. Although it is less impressive than the two horns that the African black rhinoceros carries, the great Indian rhinoceros has suffered the same fate: heavy poaching. A single rhino horn can be worth tens of thousands of dollars on the streets of India. When a poacher can make several years' salary by killing one animal, it is difficult to preach conservation to him. On the streets, the horn is shaved into paper-thin slivers and sold as an aphrodisiac and as a cure for just about every imaginable indisposition of child and adult alike. The skin of the rhinoceros, cut into strips and worn as rings, is believed by Indian Muslims to cure hemorrhoids.

Other factors, too, have conspired to reduce the rhino's numbers year by year. Human intrusion generally has done a job, including stock grazing, brush and marsh burning, the replacement of tall grasses with turf grass, the diversion or disruption of natural water courses, and diseases from cattle, especially foot-and-mouth disease. All have played their roles in making this rare and retiring animal an intruder in its own historical space.

There is a studbook for captive great Indian rhinos kept at the zoo in Basel, Switzerland. The rhino is maintained in at least thirty zoos, and several zoos have bred them with some regularity. The great Indian rhinoceros could be maintained as a species in captivity until conditions are conducive to its survival in the wild. The likelihood that this will become necessary increases with every passing year. No matter how well intentioned local conservationists are, they are being overwhelmed by human population growth that is completely out of control. More people require more space, agriculture, deforestation, and water, not to mention industry and construction. This inevitably challenges all wildlife.

A rhinoceros is a large animal whose weight is reckoned in tons, not pounds and ounces as with many other endangered species. Large animals require space and make heavy demands on their environment for food and water. They can't be tucked away in a small corner of the land and forgotten. They have to be cherished enough so that men will risk their lives tracking down poachers and courts will be harsh enough on captured poachers to make their point. Agriculturists and husbandrymen, too, are going to have to be seen to and offered meaningful alternatives to rhino habitat. No one is willing to see children starve out of love for a prehistoric beast like the great Indian rhinoceros.

As for the zoos, they are going to have to refine their art further, keep a good store of the species at hand, and follow the genetic guidelines now available. It will require a lot of science, money, and firm determination to get the great Indian rhinoceros past these hard times to a brighter future.

# Asian Small-Clawed Otter

## AONYX CINEREA

The smallest of all the world's otters is the diminutive Asian small-clawed (Aonyx cinerea). Hardly ever does it exceed ten or eleven pounds. By comparison, the river otter found in the United States and Canada runs to thirty pounds, with extreme weights of fifty pounds recorded.

Since all otters are inextricably linked to water—almost always the running water of rivers and streams—they have been very badly hit by pollution, both directly and by loss of their prey, which is anything from fish to mollusks. They have also been heavily hunted, usually trapped, for a voracious fur trade. A number of the world's otter subspecies are endangered, and an unknown number have become extinct recently. The cause of such extinction of an otter population is not always clear: Was it pollution—that is, habitat destruction—or was it trapping?

The Asian small-clawed (also known as the Oriental or Malaysian small-clawed and as the Asian clawless otter) presents something of a special problem. In the recent past the species was known to have a very wide range in southern India, and from there broadly through much of Southeast Asia all the way to Palawan in the Philippines. Today no one seems to know where small-clawed otters still exist and where they have been exterminated. Because no satisfactory survey has been made, they are not listed in the IUCN Redbook of endangered and threatened species, even though they remain a cause for concern and have been placed on other lists, including a select group of animals marked for special attention by the American Association of Zoological Parks and Aquariums.

Up until the mid-1970s, most of the small-clawed otters seen in zoos came from Thailand, where they had been sold into the pet trade, being generally tractable animals. In captivity, however, they do require special care, including a lot of running water. Most owners of small-clawed otters had become disenchanted with the work and space required by their ill-advised choice of pets and had given them up, typically to zoos. So when the Thai authorities closed the trade off in the mid-seventies, the zoos of the world found themselves with a motley collection of these interesting little animals and without any reliable data as to origin (not all came from Thailand, even those purchased there by animal dealers from other parts of Asia) and no good breeding records. Some

evidently had been breeding in captivity, but not much was known about their requirements, their reproductive biology, their genetics, or even their certain identity. Some zoologists still place the animal in a different genus, Amblonyx; as for the subspecies, it is all something of a muddle.

It is very difficult to conduct a meaningful international breeding program when most of the available parent stock of a species cannot be traced to a place of origin. At such times, mere opinion is what most zoos have to work with. When the Species Survival Plan, or SSP, was set forth in 1980, the prerequisites were that any species designated for special attention should (1) be threatened in the wild, (2) already exist in captivity, preferably in substantial numbers, and (3) already have a number of experts interested in it. In September 1981, the Asian small-clawed otter was designated as one of those special species.

These little otters do well in captivity. They have been successfully bred in zoos in places as widely dispersed as Australia, Germany, the United States, the United Kingdom, and the Netherlands, among others. Between 1985 and 1987 the captive population alone of the otters increased by 54 percent, from forty to sixty-three animals in eleven zoos, with a dozen or so others held by private collectors. But there have also been breeding failures, including spontaneous abortions, and it is possible that there is a genetic problem since a number of the otter populations that probably contributed to the present zoo collections came from islands separated for ten thousand years or more. Otters from such isolated populations may no longer be able to breed.

No one is able to determine how the small-clawed otter is doing in areas where bandits and armies have been marching and shooting almost continuously over recent history, and where scores of thousands of desperate refugees remain on the move. In areas of such human misery, wildlife is always going to get short shrift, and in the habitats of the small-clawed otter it may be decades before the situation changes. Even then, the shy, retiring little river dweller may be able to keep many of its secrets. In the meantime, clearly, precise computerized breeding records are of the greatest importance as zoos strive to fulfill one of their principal mandates: to provide haven and reproductive opportunities with genetic diversity for animals that are no longer safe in the wild.

# Koala Bear

## PHASCOLARCTOS CINEREUS

The beloved koala bear *(Phascolarctos cinereus)* is not a bear at all but a marsupial and far closer to a kangaroo or wombat than to any true bear in the world. The word "beloved" is used advisedly because few animals besides the panda, also not a bear at all, and the teddy bear, adapted fancifully from actual bears, have so captured the imagination of people everywhere.

The koala is limited in range to Australia as are most of the world's marsupials. There were once millions of koalas in the eucalyptus forests of eastern Australia, comprising three races. By 1939, they were extinct in the southern part of their range, down to an estimated one thousand animals in all of Victoria with perhaps no more than a couple of hundred remaining in New South Wales. The only stable population was in Queensland, but it numbered only ten thousand, down from a probable million at the turn of the century.

The koala is a rather slow-witted creature, completely unable to counter aggression, especially when it is launched from a high-powered rifle. In the mid-1920s Queensland permitted an open season on koalas and in 1927 over 600,000 skins were exported. Twelve years later a survey revealed that even with over a decade to recover, there were only ten thousand koalas left. The ever-voracious fur trade has continued lusting after koala skins for toys and gewgaws but they have been pretty much held at bay. Since the end of World War II, the koala has been protected and the animal is recovering in many areas natural to it.

More difficult to understand even than the fur business is the shooting koalas for sport. Hunters sight them in their rifles or just shoot the small animals out of trees as they hug the trunks, trying to be inconspicuous. They are slow moving, almost slothlike, and sleep much of the time. Their food habits make their whereabouts predictable. They can eat only the old, tough leaves of certain eucalyptus or gumtree species after the natural acids have been leached out by sun and rain.

In captivity, koalas must be fed those same leaves even if it means bringing them from a considerable distance. Most of the koalas in captivity are in zoos in Australia except those in the famed San Diego Zoo in California. A few have been born in captivity but fortunately, with a growing conservation ethic in Australia (where it has been a tough uphill battle), it may not be necessary to rely on captive collections to save the species. Fewer Australians are using koalas for target practice and the fur export business of koalas has been banned. The animal's needs for shelter and food are so specific that there is no mystery as to how to have koalas and how not to have them. If you leave them alone in their own natural habitat, they will increase.

The koala bear, with a maximum cuddle-factor working for it, almost surely has a better chance for survival in preserves than animals such as a garter snake, iguana, or some very drab little bird known only to bird-watchers. Still, the status of this attractive little marsupial must be constantly reviewed. It will never really be completely out of harm's way. It is too specialized, almost totally unadaptable to new conditions or food sources and far too easy a target as it inches along the branches of its beloved eucalyptus trees. The fur trade, too, will always be standing in the wings waiting for an opening. The cuddle-factor has never meant anything to the practitioners of that business.

# Bornean Tarsier

## TARSIUS BANCANUS

Just below the lowest of the monkeys, the marmosets, on the primate family tree come the tarsiers. They are small, athletic sprites that stay pretty much to the trees and are generally active at night although some do feed in the early morning and late evening. They look superficially like the lorises and bush-babies that are even further down in the primate lineup.

There are either three or four species of tarsiers (it is being argued) but they are all in one genus. *Tarsius.* They are restricted in range to the vast array of tiny and giant islands clustered around the Malay Peninsula. The species pictured here at Duke University's remarkable Center for the Study of Primate Biology and History is the Bornean *(Tarsius bancanus).* Its range stretches from southern Sumatra and the nearby islands Belitung and Bangka to Java and Borneo and islands near them, Karimata and Serasan and the Natuna Island group. There are no fossils giving clues to the family's original range but very closely related primates did once live in Europe and North America. That was a very long time ago. It has been a good many millions of years.

These five- to six-ounce animals are at the tail end of their evolution. Climatic changes, changing land forms, shifting plates, changing vegetation, and the evolution of both competitors and predators have conspired with time to reduce the tarsier's toehold on this planet and place them on a few isolated land masses, some of them very, very small. The tarsiers all live mainly on insects although they do manage to take a lizard occasionally. There is unlikely to be, then, a shortage of food for them if their forests are left alone. Deforestation will leave them no chance for survival in the wild, no chance at all. Some populations, such as *Tarius syrichta,* in the Philippines, have been impacted by commercial exportation even though nominally protected by law.

The status of the Bornean tarsier cannot be determined at the present time, and it may be in trouble, too. It is so retiring, is so seldom active in daylight, and keeps so entirely to thick trees that establishing even an estimate of the population is extremely difficult. When the animal is close to the edge of extinction, it may be too late to learn of its problems.

Tarsiers are rare in captivity, although the Philippine form has been bred in Stockholm. The Bornean and the Philippine are now being maintained at the Duke Primate Center. That could bode well for the future of these increasingly rare animals. It must be noted that the path to near extinction began for this remote group of primates millions of years ago. The world around them has changed too much, too often for them to make anywhere near the essential adjustments.

It is clear that the zoos of the world cannot take on every threatened or endangered species against the day when events overtake the species one by one and eliminate them from their native habitats. It would be ideal if that were possible, but there is not enough expertise, not enough space, and certainly not enough money. Those facts place the zoos and other highly specialized collections like the Duke facility in the unenviable position of having to choose. There is an element of roulette because there are so many unknowns. These unknowns include the actual status of each species thought to be in need of help, and the possibility of helping a species survive in the wild rather than in captivity by original habitat preservation, or, even under tightly controlled circumstances, by translocation. There is also the very big question of whether or not a species can survive in captivity at all. Survival means not just living out a life, but reproducing. The species needs to reproduce in more than one place to provide genetic diversity and to prevent loss from a catastrophic outbreak of disease or natural disaster.

In the absence of firm criteria that apply to all animals (and plants), it comes down to godlike decisions. Choosing can be a difficult and risky responsibility, and no one enjoys having the necessity thrust upon them. Yet that is what the zoos of the world must do.

# Orangutan

## PONGO PYGMAEUS

This greatest of the apes of Asia, the orangutan *(Pongo pygmaeus)*, is an endangered species. Its disappearance would be an incalculable loss both for science and for the cause of conservation.

The orangutan in the wild is now confined to both lowland and hill forests in areas of Indonesian Sumatra and in small pockets on Borneo, particularly in Sarawak and Sabah. Its precise range within these large areas is poorly defined. The forests are thick, and the troops of apes move. The intrusion of man, particularly deforestation, creates a fluid situation. It is estimated—hoped really—that there could be somewhere between two thousand and four thousand surviving animals, although that could be optimism rather than a census. At one time this great ape probably ranged widely on the Asiatic mainland, perhaps as far as India and possibly from central China to the Celebes.

In 1965 as an example of how things have gone, there was a war between Indonesian expansionists and Malaysian interests. The British fought on the side of the Malaysians and used artillery in forested areas, which devastated the shy apes. The small bands of apes that were there had already suffered terribly at the hands of logging crews and farmers who were clearing land for agriculture. The inoffensive orangutans simply withered in the face of such an aggressive incursion on their forest hideaway.

It is important to note that the orangutan, with an armspan of seven and a half feet or more is immensely powerful but never has represented any problem for man. The creatures are extremely retiring, never attack people except perhaps in self-defense, and even that rarely. They are about as inoffensive as an animal can be. Any assault on them is gratuitous and without purpose or excuse.

In the past, untold numbers of orangutan females were shot to get their babies away from them for a witless international animal trade. For years it ran totally out of control. What such retiring animals must have suffered in social disruption when their band or troop was attacked by men with firearms cannot even be imagined. Today, there are endless laws and conventions against that trade, and it is hoped that it has pretty well dried up.

However, rules, regulations, and agreements mean one thing in London, Berlin, San Francisco, and Stockholm but quite another in the back streets of Hong Kong, Singapore, and Kuala Lumpur. They mean absolutely nothing to poachers seeking orangutans to kidnap. All international traffic in the species, whatever the pretext, should be halted if any such activities remain. Punishment for ignoring the ban should be made as severe as possible.

There is a very good supply of orangutans in captivity. Captive births are reported from Abu Dhabi to Birmingham, Alabama. Of the hundreds of specimens in zoo collections, most of them were captive born. There hardly seems any justification for any further traffic in wild-caught animals. Perhaps if all those that remain on Borneo and in Sumatra are left in peace and if further deforestation is banned in areas where the gentle apes are found, the species may recover and hang on. In the meantime, there are substantial backups in zoos. It does seem likely, though, that future generations of men and women will have to rely entirely on zoos to know that this incredible animal lives on.

There may be a lesson in the tragedy of the orangutan. If we cannot manage our affairs on earth in such a way that our closest kin may have their modest share of this planet's resources, what is safe? If we cannot make room even for the great apes, can anything at all survive us? It is a sad matter to contemplate. Our record is a poor one indeed. It will never be understood and certainly not forgiven by future generations of human beings.

130

# Numbat

## MYRMECOBIUS FASCIATUS

The numbat *(Myrmecobius fasciatus)* has not only a genus to itself but also a family. A creature from the isolated wildlife wonderland, Australia, it is the only species in the family Myrmecobiidae. The numbat is a little animal, no more than a pound in weight, at most. It is an insect eater and seems to prefer termites over everything else.

The numbat is a marsupial, one of an incredible array of highly specialized animals that have existed in Australia and adjacent islands, such as Tasmania and to some extent on New Guinea, and just about nowhere else. The opossum, another marsupial, is widely scattered and diverse in South America; and one, the Virginia opossum, did make it to North America, but the order is pretty much an Australian exclusive.

The pretty little numbat was once widely dispersed on the Australian land mass. It is a creature of open scrub woodlands, especially in areas where the eucalyptus trees are the predominant species. It is found in or near some desert areas. The female digs a tunnel with a birthing chamber at the end, although numbats will also nest in leaves or grass on the surface or in hollow trees and logs. They will also use burrows made by other animals. The animal is generally diurnal and skitters about in abrupt jerky movements looking for food and avoiding enemies, anything from predatory mammals to snakes. It roots around, bustling, always terribly busy. It can climb trees well if it feels threatened, and there are no burrows or hollow logs at hand.

The numbers of this attractive little animal have dwindled ever since Europeans came to Australia. In New South Wales and South Australia, they are probably completely gone. They are seen in fewer numbers almost everywhere they were once common. Agriculture, with its inevitable land clearing that eliminates dead trees and fallen logs, has probably been the largest single factor in their decline. A termite-infested hollow log is a perfect habitat, providing both food and shelter. Strip mining and brush fires have taken away more land. English settlers with little zoological sophistica-

tion introduced fox, which have been unrelenting foes of the defenseless numbat. The numbat is an endangered species although it offers no competition to man on any level. Numbats don't even bite when they are caught.

Numbats are virtually unknown in zoos. Like so many of Australia's wonderful species, species no other country can boast, they could very well vanish without zoos ever being able to launch an effort to save them. There certainly is no indication now that zoos would ever be able to breed a reserve that could be used to repopulate an area made secure as an afterthought.

It is going to be very difficult to get Australians, who frankly have a somewhat frontier mentality about their spectacular and frequently unique birds, reptiles, and mammals, to give very much consideration to holding back on development to preserve their wildlife treasury. All indications are that, for this century at least, it would be a fool's errand, or at least a very frustrating project. If an Australian farmer wants to clear an area for a new crop or for husbandry, he is unlikely to change his plans because there is a tiny, banded termite eater that would prefer he didn't do it.

It may not seem fair to pick on a country or people or to single them out, because there is not a nation on earth— most assuredly not the United States—that can boast of its record with wildlife. Australia does stand out, though, for several reasons. First, other than almost totally barren Antarctica, it was the last continent into or onto which Europeans came. Also, it is the only continent that exists under one national government. For contrast, there are fifty-one nations in Africa *south of the Sahara alone.* Even North America has three nations with three sets of priorities. Finally, and this is the most critical factor, Australia has many species of wildlife no other nation on earth can display, and many more endangered and threatened species than any comparable land area. Wildlife all over the world is in trouble, it is true, but Australia has far more than its share. The numbat is but one small example.

# Red-Breasted Goose

### BRANTA RUFICOLLIS

Between a million and a million and a half years ago, a beautiful small goose lived in what is now Germany and Hungary. For some reason, probably climatic changes and possibly competition, that goose, the red-breasted goose *(Branta ruficollis)* began experiencing pressures it could handle only by retreating. Today it is primarily found in steep river valleys in the Arctic during the summer and out on the steppe grasslands of Siberia all the way to the Caspian Sea during the winter. With striking red, black, and white markings, it remains one of the most splendid of all geese.

The species probably once reached the Nile Delta with some regularity. Art found in Egyptian tombs pictures this goose; it is unmistakable with its handsome markings. There are still stragglers that get to Egypt but not very often. In fact stragglers have been reported in Greenland, Iceland, and Scandinavian countries, over much of Europe, even as far south as Italy, Iran, and Algeria—indeed a very broad area. It almost seems as if the species is fighting to regain something of the range it lost when it was forced to retreat to Siberia. That happened, we must remember, within historical times, well after the Egyptians began recording the world around them in stone friezes, memories to be taken on into the next world by the deceased. Since these geese are such attractive animals, they have been popular with zoo people and it is quite possible that some reports, at least in Europe, are of escaped zoo specimens. That is something that does happen fairly often with birds in captivity.

In the early years of serious zoo-keeping, the red-breasted goose was something of a rarity. A female, first reported on in 1853, lived on in the London zoo for years. Two captives were brought to Amsterdam in 1883 and others between then and 1906, when more began arriving from the East. The first known breeding success was at Woburn in England in 1926. After that the birds bred at Woburn, and captive populations began to build. Since wild-caught specimens of these easygoing geese settle down to a captive life after only a few days and are acknowledged as "easy keepers" that get along well with other bird species in zoo community displays, it is surprising that breeding success didn't come earlier. Dozens of red-breasted geese are successfully hatched in zoos and private waterfowl collections every year. They are popular because they are so gaudy on display, because they are a species that does not need special help, and because they are gentle, pleasant animals under virtually all conditions. They are noisy and display endlessly but are harmless. Many pairs can be kept together and mixed in with other waterfowl. They nest out in the open, often in the middle of a plain grass expanse.

It is fortunate when a species that does need help has all of these factors going for them. As much as zoo directors want to take on any species that faces problems in the wild, they do have limits to the number of species and the number of individual animals they can house, feed, and put on display. Ultimately every zoo has to face the ubiquitous problem known as the budget. It is axiomatic that any species of animal exhibited and any species of plant cultivated is done so at the expense of other candidates. Fortunately for the red-breasted goose, it is easy to manage and popular with the people who come to the zoo.

The number of people who pass through the entrance portals bring revenue with them. They often pay to park their cars, they usually pay an admission fee, and they buy food and drinks and pay for other special amenities such as zoo trains, souvenirs, and guidebooks. The money that is allocated for the zoo by a city, county, or state depends on the popularity of the institution. Very large admissions records indicate that the facility is important to the area and deserves support. It is fortuitous when animals that need help also return the favors given in captive propagation by being interesting and attractive and not labor-intensive to maintain. For the zoos charged with building population reserves against who-knows-what eventualities, animals like the red-breasted geese represent the best of all possible worlds. Well, almost the best. Truly the best would be a world where wild species did not need any help at all.

# Cereopsis Goose

## CEREOPSIS NOVAE-HOLLANDIAE

The cereopsis goose *(Cereopsis novae-hollandiae)* has anatomical clues that suggest it may be a very ancient species. It has no really close relatives today, just an extinct form from New Zealand that may have been similar. (Some cereopsis, a.k.a. Cape Barren, geese have been imported into New Zealand recently, but are not to be confused with the extinct possible-relative.)

The range of the cereopsis is limited to small islands along the southern coast of Australia. During migration, some of the geese apparently make it north to the Australian mainland where they winter in areas as remote as possible. They are handsome birds, gray overall with a whitish crown, a black tail, and black spots on the wings. Unfortunately they are also very fine tasting.

The cereopsis doesn't have any significant enemies, other than human beings, and their remote island habitats are generally intact. They are persecuted for the most part for their flesh. They have been badly overhunted, which is not an unusual report from Australia. Many Australians refuse to accept the fact that their remarkable wildlife may not always be there for the taking.

There is another reason for the persecution of this ancient goose. It eats grass, and therefore competes with sheep. Sheep farmers the world over are jealous guardians of their charges and have been notorious down through history for their treatment of wildlife. Not only do the cereopsis geese eat grass, but they taint an area with an odor that sheep apparently find repugnant.

A few cereopsis geese were presented to King George IV of England in 1830, and they were bred at Windsor and then at the London Zoo. They have been breeding in England ever since. However, cereopsis geese present a problem in captivity that has limited their numbers. They are cranky, territorial, and aggressive. They need room if more than one pair is to be kept. They will go at each other, other animals, and even human keepers if young are on the ground. They also require considerable management because they will lay their eggs in cold weather, and at times the eggs have to be taken and hatched in an incubator or placed under a broody hen inside away from the weather. Adult cereopsis geese will accept their young back if the whole thing is managed well, so propagation, although much more labor-intensive than with the red-breasted geese discussed previously, is quite possible with enough expertise. Aviculture with any species and certainly no less with waterfowl is both an art and a science.

At least fifty or so cereopsis geese are produced each year in zoos and private waterfowl collections and if the time and space were given to the project there could be more than that. The number hatched is less now than was the case before 1940. Possibly this is because the species is no longer considered that much of a challenge. The fact that the adults are really quite savage when there are young around may also account for the reduced captive production. In addition, the amount of space the cereopsis requires because of its disposition has been needed for other species as habitats all around the world have dwindled or been compromised, bringing more and more species into harm's way.

It has been demonstrated that cereopsis geese, or Cape Barren geese (both names are proper) can be bred in numbers and maintained in captivity when necessary. That in itself, coupled with a well-dispersed and substantial genetic reserve, is needed. Protection will reduce the persecution of the species off the coast of southern Australia, and the birds that have been settled in New Zealand may provide another backup. Although the cereopsis goose, with its bad smell and evil disposition, will never be one of the most popular waterfowl species on earth, there are factors in place that should enable them to survive. The backup of captive-bred populations is a comforting security measure.

# Micronesian Kingfisher

## HALCYON CINNAMOMINA CINNAMOMINA

The little Micronesian kingfisher *(Halcyon cinnamomina cinnamomina)* was once found on Guam, the home of the now seriously endangered Guam rail. With the kingfisher, though, it has gone all the way. The Guam kingfisher is now believed to be extinct in the wild. These specimens in the Cincinnati Zoo will hopefully contribute to a worldwide effort to breed captive specimens successfully enough to put a breeding nucleus back into the wild.

Another small kingfisher that apparently resembled this one was once found in the Ryuky Islands, specifically on Miyako Island, 180 miles north of the northern tip of Formosa. The last-known wild specimen of that species was reported in 1887. There are none in captivity. Other kingfishers closely akin to the Micronesian are still found in the Carolines and Palaus. This small group of birds is highly vulnerable. They need space, water to fish in, trees to nest in, fish to hunt, and no *un*natural enemies. Unfortunately, Guam can no longer guarantee the latter condition.

The imported Asian brown rat snake, the same animal that is driving the Guam rail toward extinction in the wild, preyed on the Micronesian kingfisher as well. Guam is only a little over thirty miles long. It is difficult for a tiny bird to escape an endlessly hunting enemy it did not have around as it was evolving. The snake is fast, venomous, very large, and aggressive, and arboreal as well as terrestrial. It can hunt the Guam rail on the ground or from low bushes, but it hunted the kingfisher, to extinction, in the island's dense stands of trees. Any kingfisher that learned the ways of the brown rat snake died during its lesson. A warning system could never be built into the bird's natural behavior. Long before the kingfishers could learn to be on the lookout for the snakes that were lurking everywhere to grab them, the last of the kingfishers had been taken and swallowed.

This story and the story of the Guam rail should not be interpreted as making the brown rat snake out to be some kind of ogre or villain. No less than the kingfisher that hunts living prey in the form of tiny fish, the snake is merely trying to survive. To do that it must take whatever food it can utilize. The villain of the piece is man who, out of ignorance, shifted animals around to where they were never intended to be. Eventually the brown rat snake will have so few birds and other prey to hunt that it, too, will disappear. But there is nothing man can do in the meantime that wouldn't be more damaging than the snake itself.

The story of the small Micronesian kingfisher raises a very large question. In its natural state, this bird inhabited a remote island of less than three hundred square miles. It is one of a number of small kingfishers, with other subspecies, on other islands in the same vast ocean. It is one of over eight thousand species of birds, more and more of which are getting into trouble every day. Its native home is not receptive to it, not as long as the brown rat snake still hunts there. Why should time, money, and scientific energy be put into an attempt to salvage the species?

The answer is rather like the silly question of why a man wanted to climb a mountain. "Because it is there." That really is the answer. If it is possible to save any form of life, we must make the effort. Biological diversity is this planet's greatest treasure. We caused the problem, in this case by moving animals into unnatural surroundings, and now we must see what our science can do to put Humpty Dumpty back together again. The one thing man can never do if he is to survive himself is bow to unnatural extinction. Extinction is acceptable only when it is natural. When we cause it, it is catastrophic because nothing else has evolved to replace what we have destroyed. If the zoos of the world can breed the few Micronesian kingfishers now in captivity back into a viable population, then they must do it. We have come to that point in the history of our tenure on this planet. Enough has proven to be far, far more than enough.

# Guam Rail

## RALLA OWSTONI

As recently as 1977, S. Dillon Ripley, former director of the Smithsonian Institution, wrote of the Guam rail in his now-classic monograph, *Rails of the World* (David R. Godine, publisher), "The population exploded from 21,000 before World War II to 80,000 in 1968." Then, without explanation, it is stated, "but since 1976 the species is protected." The status of the Guam rail *(Rallus owstoni)* is given as "probably not in serious danger of extermination at present, although commonly more scarce." How can the population "explode" by a factor of four but require protection?

The Guam rail is found only on Guam and perhaps a few other islands in the Marianas group. On Guam, another population has exploded, too. Someone (it *could* have been the American military) introduced a brown rat snake, presumably to control rodent pests. It came from some part of Asia, bordering on the Pacific Ocean, possibly the Philippines. No one is taking credit for the move since it was very unwise.

The brown rat snake grows to be over nine feet long, is venomous although rear-fanged, and it eats birds as well as rats. There is nothing on the island to control the snakes' population, and they are now found everywhere. Communities on Guam regularly suffer "snake-outs" from rat snakes crawling into electrical transformers and causing them to explode or burn—killing themselves, of course, in the process. The snakes, however, outnumber the transformers thousands to one.

Since Ripley prepared his monograph, the Guam rail has come close to extinction. Traditionally the Guamanians hunted the little bird for food, but things appeared to be in balance. The rails are small and prefer cover in thick brush. Depredation by the hunters was not enough to seriously impact the population. The introduction of the voracious rat snake was another matter. The rails seem unable to fly, or if they fly at all do so very poorly and certainly rarely. Snakes can go anywhere the rails can go, and since flying away doesn't appear to be an option, the birds are easily taken. A nine-foot snake can eat a lot of little birds in the course of a month, much less a year. Although the rat snakes are killed on sight, the population is growing and that of the rails is shrinking. Protection doesn't mean a thing. There are posters widely distributed on Guam asking all participants in inter-island traffic to watch for snakes and be certain none travel with cargo. But snakes don't read posters. It seems certain that with the amount of air and boat traffic between the islands, the snakes will eventually be distributed, and the last few strongholds for this little bird may be invaded and decimated.

There are very, very few Guam rails in captivity (this handsome specimen in the Cincinnati Zoo is a notable exception) and more are going to have to be captured and breeding programs established, if the species is to survive. The only alternative would be totally to eliminate the introduced brown rat snakes, and there is no acceptable way to do that presently known. The introduction of snake-eating snakes or animals such as the mongoose would compound the sin that has already been committed. Naturalist/author George Laycock has aptly labeled these introductions wildlife roulette. It almost always ends in disaster when man interferes and moves animals around, away from their natural prey or natural controls. There are notable exceptions in the ring-necked pheasant and chukkar partridge, which were brought into North America from Asia.

Since the salvation of many of the world's troubled wildlife forms will eventually depend on releases of exotic animals into new areas, a protocol for determining the possible down side of each scheme must be developed. Rhinos in Texas may not seem to offer problems because rhino populations are never huge, and the animals could easily be controlled by culling if that ever became necessary. But brown rat snakes on Guam was a terrible idea. Even feral domestic animals (goats, pigs, cats, and dogs) have proven disastrous. Mongoose are a nightmare. They eat a great deal more than cobras, almost anything they can overpower, whether wearing feathers, fur, or scales.

The brown rat snake appears to be on Guam to stay. The Guam rail almost certainly is not. Captive breeding, *perhaps* with the release of breeding nuclei on other islands without the snakes, could save the species. Or perhaps the rails on Guam simply must go, and the few other populations that exist guarded against international or accidental introduction of the snakes. It is a wildlife conservation problem with the word *emergency* stamped all over it.

# Siberian Crane

## GRUS LEUCOGERANUS

The magnificent white or Siberian crane *(Grus leucogeranus)*, as its vernacular name suggests, nests only in the Arctic reaches of Siberia. Before winter seals the region, it migrates southward to winter in northern India and occasionally Iran, western Pakistan, and China. It has accidentally appeared as far west as Sweden and on five recorded occasions at least as far east as Japan. Those geographical extremes surely were the results of severe storms or other conditions even such experienced travelers as these cranes could not handle. Over these vast migratory routes, they have regularly been harassed by hunters of every description. Scientists in their enthusiasm for museum specimens have traditionally shot far too many; and birds taken by local hunters have turned up in markets for sale along with the traditional kinds of domestic and wild fowl all along their migratory routes.

Cranes feed on small fish; reptiles, including snakes; rodents; and vegetable matter, although the white crane is not known to have been a nuisance with crops as some other crane species apparently have. Physically white cranes are large, with males up to almost twenty pounds. They have a strange whistling call that is most uncranelike. They are handsome, powerful fliers but are clearly in danger of being wiped out in the wild.

Because individual birds that are not mating in a given year may wander during the summer, and because Siberia is such a vast and remote area, real head counts are difficult to accomplish. There were once some more southerly breeding grounds, but the birds there have apparently all been eliminated. Since some move around and some do not, an accurate head count is even more difficult. So much of the land they fly above is either uninhabited or politically contested that the crane may disappear before all of its secrets are revealed.

When the cranes return to their breeding grounds, they are already paired and set about nesting and courtship activities almost as soon as they arrive. Those birds that are not going to nest that year (generally immature ones) begin their nomadic summer wanderings. It is believed that two eggs are produced by each pair but if the life-styles of the other cranes of the genus *Grus* are to be assumed for this species as well, seldom will more than one chick survive to migrate. Unlike their showy white parents, the chicks are buff-colored.

The largest single factor in the destruction of the Siberian crane is either habitat destruction or direct persecution. The principal factor may well vary from place to place, and it surely has at different times.

Fortunately, the Siberian crane can do well in captivity. There is a worldwide effort to build captive populations and the International Crane Foundation in Baraboo, Wisconsin, which has had such spectacular success with other crane species, has now been entrusted with specimens. Solid breeding populations in captivity are going to have to be established in the event the worst should happen. It has worked for the great whooping cranes, and now must be done for the others, with the Siberian crane high on the list.

One factor that will help salvage this species is that cranes are such spectacular birds, they make attractive displays for zoos although they will have to be maintained in large areas if they are expected to display, mate, and lay. Those steps, of course, are what all the effort is about. Only when the Siberian crane has been established in widely dispersed and fully controlled breeding populations can scientists and conservationists breathe easier. It won't be over then, by any means, since birds must eventually be returned to the wild before the species can be considered preserved, but the captive breeding step is the first and most important stage of the project because it is the one with the most severe time limit. If the species in the wild vanishes before captive breeding is routine, it will probably be too late for anything to matter.

In the meantime, hunters will continue to shoot them, they will appear in food stalls in village markets, and their wintering grounds will continue to be exploited for other uses. All of this may be illegal, but the law has little influence on people who are uneducated and who live in areas that are continually in a state of siege or isolated and undeveloped. The clock for the Siberian crane is ticking.

# Bali Mynah

## LEUCOPSAR ROTHSCHILDI

The beautiful white Bali mynah *(Leucopsar rothschildi)*, once known as the Rothschild mynah, is limited in its natural range to the northwestern peninsula of the island of Bali. The area is generally arid and consists of scrub and a low forest that extends up to just under four thousand feet. That extremely limited range was first recorded in 1912, and it is not known whether it was ever greater or more diverse than it is now. Much of the rest of Bali has been heavily populated by human beings for centuries, and if the mynah was driven into its present small area by human pressure, it happened a long time ago.

The Bali mynah has been protected in Indonesia since 1957. All exports to the United States of the Bali mynah since that year have been in violation of the Lacey Act, which dates back to 1900. Any specimens coming in after June 2, 1970, were also in violation of the 1969 Endangered Species Conservation Act. At least two shipments totaling fifty-five birds were refused entry at the Port of Los Angeles by importation inspectors of the United States Department of the Interior. It is believed that any shipments (and one is now known to have gotten through after June 1970) probably came through Singapore, although the supposedly complete records in Singapore do not record the events. The international traffic in endangered wildlife is notorious for three things: its extreme cruelty, its wastefulness, and the dishonesty of its record-keeping system. Mislabeling, transshipping, and faked permits are standard operating techniques. Permits are a joke, in fact, and can be bought on the open market.

The near disappearance of the beautiful white mynah from Bali is almost wholly the result of the trade in captive wildlife. Illegal and very wasteful trapping has caused the deaths of untold thousands of birds. Since the animals are usually being smuggled for at least some stage of their journey, they are crammed into very small containers. The people handling them are less than skilled aviculturists, and the captives are subjected to intolerable weather and temperature extremes and denied food and water for long periods. The inevitable loss under these conditions is considered natural and unavoidable by the practitioners.

Now for the ironic part. Hundreds and hundreds of Bali mynahs have been bred in the world's zoos. It is one of the great success stories of modern bird-keeping. Some individual zoos have recorded well over a hundred successful hatchings, and there are over a hundred zoos with breeding pairs in their collections. There is absolutely no reason further to impact the very limited wild population. All that could ever be needed can be and are in fact being produced by zoos around the world.

Very often captive birds, and mammals and reptiles for that matter, present a problem when it comes to diet. Not so this mynah from the rough north of Bali. A diet designed for soft-billed birds is easily concocted in the form of concentrated greenish-brown pellets made from meat by-products, cereal, liver, egg, casein, and fats. On this diet, and perhaps others like it used by different zoos in other parts of the world, the birds regularly form their pair bonds, display, and produce two or three eggs, which both parents incubate for a period of twelve to fourteen days. The nestling period lasts for twenty-one to twenty-six days.

Second-generation breeding is no longer a novelty with the Bali mynah, and there is more than enough genetic material to spread around in the form of breeding loans, out-and-out trades, even gifts from the larger, well-endowed zoos to smaller ones with a good record of aviculture. There can be a second hundred zoos and some of the very fine private collections involved within the decade. Now Indonesia must lean heavily on anyone molesting the much-reduced wild stock for any reason whatsoever. Places like Singapore, with the proverbial blind eye and deaf ear when it comes to commerce in any form, must join the ranks of the concerned. It is easy to save the Bali mynah as a wild-living bird in a distant land, at least when compared with other species. The question is, will we do it?

# Indian Cobra

## NAJA NAJA

In most people's minds the Indian cobra *(Naja naja)* is the dramatic prototype of the dangerous, sacred, mysterious, and evil serpent that spreads its "head" and spits its venom, whose bite is almost instantly and inevitably fatal. Checking off the errors in that fictional but widely held image: the death rate from the bite of the Indian cobra is about 4.9 percent; so much for inevitably fatal. Except under the most extraordinary circumstances, the venom is slow acting; and death, if it is to come, will take many hours or even days. The Indian cobra does not spit its venom: some African cobras do, but they are very different animals. The snake does not spread its "head" but actually the ribs behind its head in order to make the snake appear larger than it is and hopefully drive away a foe before a physical encounter is necessary. Snake fangs, venom glands, and venom constitute what is primarily a food-getting sytem, and the snakes know instinctively to avoid wasting it on its secondary use, self-defense. Hence the classic cobra's hood is simply a bluff.

Unfortunately, there is another bit of nonsense about Indian cobras, which is that the supply is endless. Cobras are persecuted because they are seriously venomous and because they can be a nuisance when they lay their eggs behind the rows of books in the public library. When they come around homes and places of business looking for rodents, there can be unfortunate encounters, and it is all but impossible to get much sympathy for them. Like all snakes, they startle people by suddenly appearing, and that is not readily forgiven.

Cobras are caught and exported for a weird pet trade. Most of them die in transit or shortly after arrival. They die if their fangs and venom glands are surgically removed, so there is no way to make a cobra into a suitable pet. Cobras also die by the tens of thousands to serve the skin game with yet one more exotic leather for wallets, shoes, handbags, and attaché cases. Pigskin properly prepared and stamped is virtually indistinguishable from reptile skin. It is certainly close enough to serve the purpose.

There are many kinds of cobras from many places in Africa and Asia and the Middle East. Because it is so difficult to get sympathy for cobras no matter where they come from, even animal "lovers" and part-time conservationists who like to pass judgment on what is worthy of attention and what is not, will often be heard to say the cobras not only can but should go. That is not biologically sound. Cobras of any kind, no less than any other animals, are important species with a job to do. They kill millions of potentially harmful, or at least wasteful, rodents each year where there is simply not enough food to go around, much less to waste. As for the rodents and their well-being, they evolved to live in a world with cobras, and their reproductive rates anticipate predation. As the predation is cut back, the rodents run wild.

If the cobra in India and elsewhere is not left alone, at least in areas where it is not a threat to human well-being, they will wither away like any other animal and vanish with terrifying suddenness, leaving an unfortunate void. No one suggests that a nest of cobras in the basement of a nursery school should go unmolested. Cobra venom, incidentally, probably has extensive beneficial medical properties and if the cobras go, so will their highly complex neurotoxins. Much research remains to be done.

There are Indian cobras and many other kinds of cobras as well in zoos all over the world. Many zoos have had captive clutches of eggs hatch regularly. There is little doubt that the species could be kept going in captivity with expert curatorship, but zoos are not where cobras are needed most. They have a necessary role to play in the natural world. The lands they inhabit would be very different without them and it could come to that in the near future over much of the cobra's range.

# Fiji Banded Iguana

## BRACHYLOPHUS FASCIATUS

This handsome species of lizard from the remote Fiji and Tonga Islands in the Pacific Ocean, the Fiji banded iguana *(Brachylophus fasciatus),* is the kind of animal that could slip away almost unnoticed. Indeed, species like it are becoming extinct at a terrifying rate around the world. Fortunately the Fiji Islands, remote as they are, are now a tourist haven, and both island groups have been known by zoologists for a great many years. Remote island groups are always interesting to both zoologists and botanists because of the unique species they spawn. That interest goes back at least to Darwin and his work in the Galapagos Archipelago.

Shortly before World War I, the beautiful iguana of the Fiji and Tonga Island groups was reported as "common." But it has apparently been straight downhill since then. It is now considered rare everywhere and is almost certainly extinct on a number of individual islands in both groups.

A number of factors have contributed to the species' demise. Mongooses have been established on many of the islands as a dangerous exotic. These fast and fearless little mammals hunt iguana eggs and both young and adult specimens as well. An iguana has little hope of defending itself against a marauding mongoose. A form of cane toad has also been introduced to many of the islands where the iguana once flourished and they, too, are a major threat, but in a totally different way. The iguanas attempt to eat the toads, which are poisonous, as so many amphibians are. The iguanas that die from eating cane toads have no way of passing that critical information along to their young. If the Fiji iguanas had the time, space, and numbers to survive for centuries, they would automatically be subject to natural selection. Those that hunted toads would not live to reproduce and those that did not hunt toads would. But the Fiji iguana does not have time, space, or numbers.

The Fijians also persecute iguanas and often kill them on sight. The people of these islands need to be educated to the fact that the lizards are harmless, unique, and of great interest to science. Forest clearing on the islands is also limiting habitat and further pushing the lizards toward final destruction. It is the endlessly recurrent theme heard all over the world.

There is little hope of ridding the islands of cane toads and mongooses where they have become established. The future of the species really must depend on outlying islands where neither exotic is present to hunt the lizard or poison it as it in turn hunts for a living.

The Fijian banded iguana can live in captivity; the San Diego Zoo, at least, reports captive reproduction. It is doubtful that the half-a-dozen zoos that have successfully maintained the species could keep it going without a very concentrated effort. Unfortunately iguana have neither the "sex appeal" of great impressive animals like lions, tigers, elephants, and rhinoceros nor the "cuddle factor" of chimpanzees and koala bears. They come from a distant place far out of the mainstream of most people's experience. Although there is romance in the names of Fiji and Tonga Islands, it remains to be seen whether that romance will rub off on a lizard.

Fortunately, the Fiji banded iguana is a handsome animal. Where we concentrate our conservation dollars and efforts often depends on things as tenuous and subjective as that. The irony is not lost on the people who have devoted their lives to saving as many plants and animals as possible without resorting to a beauty contest before making decisions and putting forth their best efforts.

# Komodo Dragon

## VARANUS KOMODOENSIS

The awesome Komodo dragon *(Varanus komodoensis)* is the largest lizard in the world by a very wide margin. Alligators and crocodiles are distinctly not lizards! A really big male can be ten feet long and weigh in the vicinity of three hundred pounds. That is probably very close to being a record animal, however. The genus *Varanus* is distinguished by the size range it represents. There is this monster, and then there is a short-tailed Australian lizard *(Varanus brevicauda)* that doesn't exceed eight inches and whose weight is measured in ounces. The Komodo dragon is nothing more nor less than a very, very big monitor lizard.

The range of the so-called dragon is one of the most restricted in the world. It is found on Komodo and possibly still on Rintja Islands, parts of Indonesia formerly known as Dutch Sunda Islands. There were probably populations on several other islands in the area, but they have been extirpated. Since these lizards are powerful swimmers and since there is an eastward-flowing current, the Torres, coming to the islands from Australia, the Komodo monitor may have island-hopped over that great distance over a long period of time. There was once an animal quite like it in Australia, but it has long since vanished as it very well may have on intermediate islands along the Torres Current route.

The Komodo monitor or dragon prefers open country and hunts endlessly for carrion. It will kill its own prey, however, anything from deer to feral pig and, it is feared, human beings. On the one or two islands they still inhabit, these gigantic monitor lizards appear to have no natural enemies. There is a clear and present danger to their survival, however. Komodo Island is roughly twelve by twenty miles, not a very large land mass. Natives from Timor, badly in need of protein, come to Komodo Island to hunt the feral pigs and deer, too. Young Komodo monitors can survive on birds' eggs and beetle grubs, but the massive adults require far more substantial prey than that. If their prey is too far reduced, the monitors will be as well.

It would be an ironic twist if a species not directly destroyed by man in a habitat that is pretty well intact died out. Death would come to the species because man competed with it as a hunter, seeking the same prey. Man has some options, but the monster monitor lizard from Indonesia does not.

Were the species to try and establish itself on other islands, those inhabited by man, it would be directly destroyed. The animals woud eventually take domestic stock, reduce wildlife species needed by man, and possibly represent a danger to children and elderly people.

There is a second irony in the conflict between the Komodo dragons still surviving and man. Unchecked, the natives of Timor would very soon eliminate both the deer and the feral pig population of Komodo Island and stop going there for protein. In the meantime, to no real end, the monitors will have been starved into extinction. The only possible way of preserving the giant lizards is to raise the living standards of the people on Timor. People can not be left to battle wildlife for food—not if the people or the wildlife are to survive.

The rare Komodo dragon does survive in six to ten zoos from time to time, but the number and longevity of captive specimens are not impressive; nor is breeding success, which stands at about zero. This is a remarkable species, representing true giantism and it does have a great deal of appeal as a zoo display species, but so far there has been very little success with it. It is a species where translocation may be absolutely essential. It would be of enormous help if the zoos could help supply the stock.

Several things may have to be done simultaneously. Specimens may have to be captured on Komodo Island and moved to other islands with a good prey base. Prey animals may have to be released on Komodo Island to breed and provide food for the dragons. The people of Timor must be given alternatives for protein. If the zoos could at the same time solve the problems of maintaining and successfully breeding the species, it could still have a chance. Failing the success of this multipronged offensive, we could see the largest lizard to survive into historical times vanish.

150

WESTERN HEMISPHERE

# Golden-Headed Tamarin

## LEONTOPITHECUS ROSALIA CHRYSOMELAS

The tiny monkeys known as marmosets and tamarins (family Callitrichidae) are limited to tropical Central and South America. Arboreal in habit, they hold to forests and wooded areas on some savannas within that range. They are the lowest true monkeys on the primate family tree, with seventeen species. Conditions are not good for any of these.

The golden-haired tamarin *(Leontopithecus rosalia chrysomelas)* shown here is in the Los Angeles Zoo. There is also a golden lion tamarin and a golden-rumped tamarin, along with many other tamarins, in addition to the marmosets. In the wild, the golden-headed tamarin's range is limited to Bahia State in southeastern Brazil. It occurs only in coastal forests and has become more and more limited to small isolated pockets. It is extremely vulnerable. Its habitat is being destroyed in schemes demanding deforestation. Most of the specimens that remain are on private land, much of which is coca plantations, where realistic control is out of the question. Unless private landowners want to save this small primate—and none, apparently do—there is nothing that can be done but remove the few that are left from harm's way.

There are not many held in zoos anywhere, and reproduction, while it has occurred, is much the exception. There is nothing like a viable breeding nucleus to keep this species from extinction if the worst were to happen in the wild. The problem is the worst seems to be happening. The small monkey's life-style makes it extremely difficult to find. Many of the pockets where it might be holding on are difficult to reach and generally on privately owned property, so a meaningful census is all but impossible to accomplish. With the wild population so difficult to assess, and with so few in institutions, this species could simply vanish while zoologists stand helplessly by.

It is unlikely that the coastal forests of southern Brazil can be made safe unless at least one major preserve area comes into being and whatever wild stock there is is translocated to a place where it can live under blanket protection.

The little golden-headed tamarin was first described by scientists in 1820, but there is no way of determining if it was known to people outside of the area before that. Since that time, very few specimens have been collected. This may mean the animal has always been rare and perhaps even on the road to extinction for over a century and a half. Twenty years ago it was estimated that there were between four and five hundred specimens still in the wild. At that time, there was a single specimen in captivity, in the Rio de Janeiro Zoo. It has never really looked promising for this species.

There is inherent hazard in justifying concern for a particular species because that implies a hierarchy or at least the intervention of human opinion or choice. A tamarin in Brazil, a rhinoceros in Kenya, a garter snake near San Francisco are all cause for enormous concern. There are, however, some special circumstances that should be noted. They do not suggest one species is more important than another, but these special circumstances can explain why a particular species is of concern for reasons beyond its inherent right to survive and our eternal need for biological diversity.

The special interest in the golden-headed tamarin is that primates in general have been declining in numbers and species for centuries. They have vital secrets about not only their physical evolution but about ethology, or the evolution of their behavior. In all of this world, we have only the seventeen Latin American species of the Callitrichids. Although fossil records for such small animals that have always been forest dwellers is disappointing, we may assume that what we have are remnants. They are first on line on the monkey scale as it ascends up from the lemurs and before that from the lorises. To lose them would be to lose a vital link in a sequence of events that led to the great apes and eventually to us, not necessarily (almost assuredly not) in a straight line, but it is our tree as well as theirs. That does not say, again, that it would be worse to lose this remote and diminutive primate from far down in South America than it would be to lose the Bengal tiger or the European bison, but it does remind us that none of this business of habitat destruction and extinction of plants and animals can be taken as inevitable or just plain "too bad."

154

# Red Uakari

CACAJAO CALVUS RUBICUNDUS

The red uakari *(waa-kari) (Cacajao calvus rubicundus)* is a New World monkey, another animal whose very existence hangs in the balance because of the relentless assault being made on them both directly and on their native tropical forests. It is patently obvious that some animals have evolved to live in very precise habitats. Their demands are exacting because of the food they need, their social organization, their locomotive styles and skills, and their means of dealing with predators. High on this list of specialists are the monkeys. Some, like the baboons of Africa, live as easily on the open savanna as in brush or forest, while others, like the three uakari, red, white, and black, simply cannot be far from forested land for any length of time. Everything they were evolved to need is there and nowhere else.

All the monkeys and apes of the world with the single exception of the douroucouli, or night monkey *(Aotus trivirgatus)*, also a South American species, are diurnal. They go down when the sun does and cannot take advantage of darkness to move around and feed. That makes them easy prey, all the more so if they cannot climb high up in the trees at the first hint of a stalking predator. Monkeys usually escape upward, in a vertical, or at least steeply diagonal, flight path. Only when they are well above the ground do they utilize horizontal flight.

In its surviving native range, the region between the Amazon and Putumay Rivers in western Brazil and eastern Peru, and only in the tropical humid forest (*not* the subtropical rainforest or cloud forest), the red uakari must contend with jaguar, cougar, ocelot, and margay as well as the large constricting snakes. If it goes to a river to drink, there are caiman waiting. Almost everywhere, there is danger from lurking humans on a variety of destructive errands. It is a hazardous life, and flight into dense, high vegetation is its only salvation. There are new human settlers in the Amazon region, who hunt the red uakari for skins, souvenir collections, for food, and even for a limited trade in the pet market. Laws in both Brazil and Peru have limited the export of uakari for the pet trade, but local people and the burgeoning population of newcomers can collect them for meat with little fear of retribution.

In the past, hunting appears to have been the major cause of the monkey's decline; however, unquestionably that factor has been overtaken by the newer, more insidious broad-front assault of deforestation. Of course, these factors inevitably combine. The fewer trees left standing, the more exposed the monkeys will be and the more crammed into ever smaller areas. When there are no avenues left by which the uakari can travel from one forested patch to another, the isolated animals will have no chance at all.

The monkeys of the world, although highly intelligent and even inventive, generally do not adapt well. They are among the world's specialists, and once the native range of an animal like the red uakari, or any of the three forms, in fact, has been severely altered, the animal is probably doomed as a wild-living species. The uakari are exhibited in very few zoos, and there is a serious question about further impacting wild populations by trapping more and exporting them from Brazil and Peru. The rare specimen shown here is from the Los Angeles Zoo, one of the few institutions to exhibit the species.

The uakari have so far failed to breed in zoos in sustaining numbers, certainly not frequently enough to be very encouraging. Zoos may not be an option for this species or its two cogenitors, the black uakari and the white (or bald). It may prove to be absolutely necessary to salvage large areas of unmolested forest with well-forested avenues for transit between them so isolated pockets don't form. Isolation offers a second hazard: the inability of the animals to spread their genes around. Isolated pockets inevitably become dangerously inbred, as sure a road to extinction as hybridization or direct destruction of the monkeys themselves. Another major hazard exists when prey animals are isolated: their predators are isolated, too, in the same islands of forest. With an increasing human threat, cats and snakes are as endangered by exposure as monkeys. Eventually the hunters will consume all of their prey and then die of starvation. It is a vision of hell on earth: all natural relationships destroyed and the biological diversity that makes this planet special diminishing by the hour. It is truly the present ignoring the past and stealing from the future.

# Cotton-Top Tamarin

## SAGUINUS OEDIPUS

Just above the tarsiers and lorises in the primate hierarchy and below the family Cebidae, the New World monkeys, comes the family Callitrichidae, the seventeen species of marmosets and tamarins.

It is often said that marmosets and tamarins are less intelligent than either the Old or New World monkeys, but that is difficult to establish. They have different temperaments, and because of their extremely small size, as small as five ounces in some species, they have relatively more to fear.

The Callitrichidae are swift, intense, and alert. They jump and leap and skitter along branches. All but one species from the Matto Grosso are almost entirely arboreal. That one species, the silvery or black-tailed marmoset *(Callithrix argentata)*, will take to tall grass to hide and nest.

The cotton-top tamarin *(Saguinus oedipus)* pictured here is a forest animal from Colombia, Costa Rica, and Panama, well north of the ranges of most of the other species. The species in this genus are also known as long-tusked marmosets. They are very family-oriented. The male assists in the birth and carries the one or two young, except when they are feeding. He will stand by when the young are nursing and then relieve the female of the burden. They are extremely alert little sprites with excellent hearing and eyesight, and probably a keen sense of smell. Like all of the others in their family, they are agile and quick moving.

Man is one enemy the cotton-top tamarin can't escape. No amount of agility and speed can avoid the consequences of the chain saw and the torch. Throughout most of this primate's range, there has been endless deforestation, cutting, slashing, and burning to market lumber and to clear land for sugarcane and other crops. Land that held a tropical forest of immense diversity and complexity, up to two hundred plant species per acre, ironically makes poor agricultural land. About all that can be expected of the soil is a few good years, if that. Any forest that is left will eventually creep back over the pillaged land. It might take a century, but the forest in most of its diversity could come back. But there is no sign that the present rape mentality is about to turn that 180-degree corner. Some species of plants and invertebrates are so specialized and have such limited ranges that they will become extinct, most of them, before we can even iden-

tify them. They will have come and gone without our ever knowing their worth to the animals of the forest and perhaps even to us.

Fortunately, the cotton-top tamarin breeds extremely well in captivity. Although officially listed as an endangered species because of the probable future of its forest home and its already very much reduced range, there are between seven hundred and a thousand in zoos now with hundreds born every year. One of the peripheral impacts that did such a terrible job on the species was trapping for the international animal trade. That is no longer necessary. There is more than enough genetic diversity and plenty of breeding stock so zoo populations between sales, exchanges, and breeding loans can be totally self-sustaining.

The marmosets, because they do not require very large enclosures, are attractive zoo display animals. Despite their size, they are hardy as long as they are not exposed to very cold weather or sudden temperature changes. Kept in a warm, moist environment and given a proper diet that is now well understood by zoo professionals, these small primates can do very well.

A big question arises, however. Will zoos have to hold the tamarin and its kin for another century or more before there is forest secure enough in countries politically stable enough for them to wander safely through the trees? Indeed, that may be the case. There is also the question of what a century or more in captivity might do to these animals. Will they retain the necessary survival skills and know what to eat, where to drink, and what sounds, smells, and shadows to avoid? We do not know.

Recently another species, the golden lion tamarin, was collected from nineteen zoos around the world and, after conditioning at the National Zoo in Washington, D.C., was released in a forested preserve in Brazil. It was the first primate successfully restored and was a pilot project. Not long after the release, a devastating fire broke out, and much of the preserve was destroyed. The impact on the fledgling tamarin population had to be extremely bad. It will take some time to assess the true damage. Too many animals of an endangered species in too small an area can be a very dangerous thing.

# Grizzly Bear

## URSUS ARCTOS HORRIBILIS

There are two approaches to taxonomy, the scientific naming of wildlife. Proponents of these approaches are sometimes called the *lumpers* and the *splitters.* Until recently the splitters described the grizzly bears of North America and the brown bears of Alaska (including the Kodiak Island and Alaskan Peninsula populations), as well as the brown bears of Europe and Asia, as sixty-four different species. The last word is probably not yet in. Currently, however, the lumpers hold sway and consider all these bears to be one species with many subspecies and geographical races.

The grizzly bears (generally listed as subspecies *Ursus arctos horribilis*) once had a vast range from Mexico to the Arctic circle in Canada and Alaska. They have probably always been limited to North America in their present form. But as the continent was settled, the great, gruff, and frequently aggressive bears had to give ground. Men on horses, with rifles and packs of dogs, were far more than even an eight-hundred-pound grizzly could survive. Indians afoot with bows and spears were easier to avoid or eliminate when an encounter took place.

The Mexican grizzly is just about finished, if it is not already gone. In California, where it once had a very good population, the grizzly was exterminated in 1922. There are certainly geographical races of grizzlies but whether there are, or more accurately were, really more than one subspecies is yet to be sorted out.

The grizzly in northern Canada and in Alaska will probably hang on for many years because it is a regulated trophy animal and is hunted presumably under firmly controlled conditions. In the lower forty-eight states, there are some grizzlies in a few national parks or other reasonably natural areas but the pressure to eliminate them is unrelenting because accidents do occur. Because of their very poor eyesight, they are easy to surprise if the wind is from them to you, and a startled grizzly bear can spoil a camper or hiker's whole day. How long they will last in the southern parts of their range is difficult to estimate but probably not for long.

Grizzly bears do well in captivity and reach ages probably never attained in the wild, twenty years and more. They can and do breed in captivity although surprisingly few are kept in a relatively small number of zoos. They take a lot of space because they are essentially loners and many will not share a captive habitat without fighting to the death. Males in captivity have been known to kill females offered to them as mates. It takes careful curatorship because, although bears raised as infants by humans can become amazingly tractable and even affectionate, under normal zoo conditions they are generally quite dangerous. Still, if the need arises, grizzlies can be maintained as a species in captivity.

Returning grizzlies to the wild at some distant future date could offer problems that may be all but insurmountable. The mother or sow keeps her cubs with her for a year and sometimes two. There is a lot of learning on the part of young bears while in their mother's care. How well young bears fare without having had an experienced sow to train them under natural, wild conditions is not fully understood. Certainly any bear conditioned not to fear man, even the faintest whiff of man (bears really believe only their noses), is a bear that is not going to survive long. In virtually all of their former range, the word that a grizzly bear had returned would bring forth a battery of guns and dogs. Every hunter in the world, it seems, wants to kill the legendary grizzly and have its skin, head attached, on their den floor or wall.

Bears, although carnivores by tooth structure, disposition, and digestive system, are very flexible when it comes to food. They do kill everything from squirrels and rabbits to deer and elk (and, unfortunately, livestock when that is an available alternative). They also fish and eat berries, grass, and other vegetable matter. Because of their enormous bulk and also because they fast from early winter until late spring, they spend much of their time eating from late spring through the fall months. They can survive in a variety of habitats from dense forest to open plains to Arctic tundra. It is not adaptability that is their problem. It is man with his dogs and rifles. As long as grizzly bears are still in the wild in good numbers, as they are in Alaska and Canada, the zoos of the world can keep their somewhat relaxed attitude toward them and display them only as a matter of pleasing their visitors. It may not be too long, however, before zoos will have to show increased interest as these great brown carnivores disappear from even the northernmost parts of their range.

# North American Bison

BISON BISON

The saga of the North American bison *(Bison bison)* is one of the best-known conservation stories in history. It is the story of near tragedy, profound concern, concerted effort, and final triumph.

Before Europeans began spreading westward out onto the Great Plains of the American and Canadian west, there were an estimated 60 to 100 million bison roaming in vast herds from northern Alberta to the southwestern parts of the United States, and eastward as woodland bison to Pennsylvania.

There is a lovely myth that the American Indians who based their culture on the bison were tremendous natural conservationists. That is almost certainly not true. They, too, saw those endless herds as indestructible. There are many remains to show where entire herds were stampeded over cliffs and killed in numbers that could never have been utilized by the number of Indians at hand.

The reasons why there were so many bison present when the Europeans arrived, despite the fact that the Indians had built their very existence around them for centuries, is that before the European arrived, the Indians did not have firearms. Even more significantly, there were very few Indians. The nomadic bands and clans were small and widely scattered. The bison were simply overpowering in number.

But then the explorers arrived, the railroad tracks were laid, and the European "sportmen" followed. Excursion trains bristled with rifles as these sportsmen fired into the herds without ever setting foot on the ground. The more adventuresome were met by outfitters and rode out into the herds killing without purpose. Millions of bison were slaughtered for their hides, which were popular as lap robes back east. Millions more were killed for their tongues alone, which were considered delicacies and were salted, kegged, and shipped back on the same trains that brought the recreational killers to the scene.

As the twentieth century approached, the unthinkable had happened. The American bison was nearing extinction. They could no longer be counted in the tens or scores of millions but in the few hundreds. The great American bison herds were finished.

In haste and perhaps in near panic, the American Bison Society was formed in New York City, at the New York Zoological Society in the Bronx. Captive animals were collected from small zoos and private ranches and slowly, in appropriate locations, small herds were rebuilt. Breeding nuclei were established on private land holdings and in zoo collections. Those small bands have never stopped growing, and today the United States and Canada have as many bison as they have room for. There is one wild herd, near Great Slave Lake in northern Alberta, Canda, but all of the rest are descendants of the few hundred animals the American Bison Society saved from the brink of extinction. A couple of hundred plains bison are born in zoos every year and even a few of the much rarer woods bison *(Bison bison athabascae)* are, too. The European bison or wisent is a different story and it is told elsewhere in this book.

Bison herds now roam in parks and preserves in many parts of Canada and the United States. Some are bred to domestic cattle to produce animals known as *beefalos*. A controlled number of bison are slaughtered each year and their meat is sold commercially. The number of animals at any one time is a matter of the space and resources private organizations and state and federal governments want to allot to them. There will never again be 60 to 100 million bison thundering across the American west, and indeed there is no reason why there should be. The species has been preserved by controlled, captive breeding. Animals have been returned to open spaces and, although they are still controlled, they are in a very real sense wild. Foreign zoos have and can get all they need whenever they want them. If there is a total success story, it is the story of the New York Zoological Society, the American Bison Society, and the species that care and concern brought back from oblivion to become a permanent part of the land they once dominated.

# San Joaquin Kit Fox

## VULPES MARCOTIS

The kit fox (*Vulpus marcotis*, although it could be a subspecies of the more easterly swift fox, *Vulpes velox*, a taxonomic nicety yet to be settled) is the smallest of all North American canines and one of the smallest members of the dog family in the world. A full-grown specimen may weigh from three to six pounds, which makes it about the size of a small house cat. A nine- to-twelve-inch tail, a bushy coat, and large "batlike" ears make it seem larger than it really is.

The kit fox can be described as beneficial because of the number of rodents it eats. The rodents evolved with that natural attrition built into their reproductive rate. If the kit fox disappears, the rodents will continue to reproduce at the same rate and perhaps to irreparable harm to the fragile environment.

The kit fox is a nocturnal animal, coming out at dusk to hunt small desert rodents like the kangaroo rat. It keeps pretty well to its burrow during the day and avoids the worst of the desert heat. It prefers open, sandy ground, the more level the better. It will live around low desert vegetation such as juniper.

Although the desert is often referred to as a harsh environment, like the tundra or the mountaintop, it is a natural environment and may seem harsh only to species not evolved to live there, species like man. For the kit fox the desert is perfectly natural and right, just as the Arctic is to the polar bear and the Antarctic is to the penguin and the Weddell seal. This business of declaring all areas where we do not naturally reside with ease as *harsh* downgrades them. The desert is a perfectly fine environment, very supportive of desert species. Any other view of them is egocentric.

The kit fox, like its virtually exact counterpart, the fennec of North Africa, the Sinai and Arabian Peninsulas, is well equipped for desert life. If it is out of its cool, moist burrow during the day, it moves slowly and seeks shade as often as possible, when evaporation is at its highest point. Its feet are furred on the bottom except for the toe pads, which give it better traction when it trots back and forth across the sand during the nighttime hours. Its large ears contribute to very acute hearing and may, it has been suggested, act as a cooling system to disperse body heat. Like all desert-dwelling carnivores, the kit fox gets much of the moisture it needs from the prey it takes. It is interesting to note that the kit fox is the only member of the Carnivora in North America, evolved solely for life in the desert. All of the others—cougar, gray fox, badger, bobcat, coyote, wolf—all are found well away from desert areas as well. Not so the kit fox.

Over much of its remaining range, the kit fox is in trouble. Long trap lines that in many cases are seldom checked have made terrible inroads into the populations of this trusting little fox. It will come right into a camp at night and accept food put out for it. More than one trekker has awakened in the morning to find the catlike footprints of the kit fox all around his sleeping bag. A trap set for bobcat or badger will easily destroy the tiny fox of the desert night.

Even worse has been predator control—efforts to rid areas of coyote, cougar, or other larger hunters. Poison baits are soon come upon by the curious kit fox and it takes very little "1080" or strychnine to end a kit fox's career as a desert ratter. There are whole sections of the kit fox's range where sightings have become a rarity. The kit fox is tiny, vulnerable, and an inveterate busybody. It easily succumbs to heavy-handed devices of destruction like poison and traps.

There are a few kit foxes in zoos, but since they are nocturnal, any zoo exhibiting them requires a nocturnal animal facility, a special building with self-contained exhibits, darkened passageways for visitors, and red lights in the animal areas. Without these special installations, the kit foxes would never be seen. Animals that can't be seen are seldom maintained by zoos except for research and special propagation assignments.

A few kit foxes are born in captivity but so far there have been far too few to make the captive population anywhere near self-sustaining. If there is much further degradation of desert habitats in North America—mining, urban sprawl, waste disposal, highway, resort and housing development, military use for maneuvers, artillery impact zones and bombing zones for the Air Force, irrigation and land reclamation—this species could simply vanish. Its spread on a map from Oregon to Mexico is deceptive. Its actual range is discontinuous and much of it is under constant assault. Neither the zoos nor the state or federal government are prepared for a crash in this animal's population.

# Cougar

## FELIX CONCOLOR

The cougar *(Felis concolor)* has the greatest north-south range of any species of cat in the world—from southern Canada to Patagonia in southern Argentina. It also has more names in the English language than just about any cat: cougar, puma, mountain lion, panther, painter, American lion, red lion, and a good many more regional nicknames that most of us wouldn't recognize. They are all interchangeable. The important point is that, under all of these names in all of that vast range, it is still that single species of cat.

As for habitat, cougar are found in the deserts of the southwestern United States, on the steppes of South America, in the swamps of Florida, and perhaps still Georgia, in the mountains and high meadows of Oregon and Utah, in the forests of California and New Brunswick, in the Canadian Maritimes, and in the jungles of Central and South America. The cougar is one of the most adaptable of all of the world's large predators. If it were as small as a red fox or even a coyote, it would undoubtedly be in the suburbs of many major American cities. It is large, and it leaves big pugmarks. Average size for an active, mature animal is probably between 125 and 150 pounds. Those pugmarks and the cat's inevitable appetite make it difficult for the cougar to keep its presence a secret.

Unfortunately, cougars like horse meat, and the species has been in trouble with man since man first arrived in cougar country. It has always been heavily hunted out of spite, in largely imagined self-defense, and as a trophy. It is trapped, used in guaranteed controlled hunts, hunted with dogs (the usual way), poisoned, kept as a pet (usually fatal to the cats), and abused in just about every way man knows to abuse wildlife. There is no doubt that some mountain lions have killed livestock, but nowhere near the extent claimed by some ranchers. The persecution of the cat has far exceeded any real need, and the results have been predictable and unfortunate. The cougar will take carrion when it can find it and gets blamed for kills it never made.

In all of the North American southeast, there are probably no more than twenty-five to thirty "panthers" left. (In Florida, the cat is known as *panther* or *painter*.) In the Canadian Maritime Provinces, there may be none or there may be a couple of dozen. Cougars are so secretive it is all but impossible to get anything but opinions, guesses, and folk tales. Over most of the cat's North American range, it has vanished, extirpated by hunting and trapping. In some parts of North America, it holds on and even does rather well, especially in Oregon, Idaho, and Utah. It still can be found in small numbers in California and several other western and southwestern states. There are endless claims for Maine, Tennessee, West Virginia, and many other places. Most of the reports, however, are fanciful.

Reports of attacks on human beings by wild cougars are extremely rare, and have almost inevitably involved immature cats nearly dead from starvation—cats who apparently lost their mothers before really learning to hunt. In one case where a human being killed the attacking cat with a shovel, it weighed less than twenty-five pounds. The cougar is so retiring it is not a threat to man. Virtually all stories to the contrary have been excuses for man attacking the cougar.

Unfortunately, the guaranteed hunt has come into being. It is a staged event. The cats are usually trapped in Latin America and shipped north. There they are held in cages while the outfitter runs his sportsman around in circles for as many days as the outfitter feels appropriate. At a preset time the cat is released where the dog pack can get its scent. The dogs run it up a tree, and the sportsman shoots it off its branch. Little wonder there is a guarantee that "no cat, no fee"!

At least fifty zoos produce anywhere from 150 to two hundred cubs a year. There is no trouble at all in breeding this cat, the problem comes in containing it. Like the leopard, and to some extent the jaguar, the cougar is a superb athlete. Enclosures with heavy gage tops are not sufficient. It is extremely unfair to keep an animal like the cougar in a small cage, but larger areas must be enclosed with serious fencing. No zoo welcomes the prospect of escapees and the resultant publicity.

How long the cougar can hang on in the wild is a matter of opinion. It will vanish from some pockets very soon, but may hang on in others well into the next century. The zoos have good reserves, and this is a cat you are far more likely to see in a zoo than in the wild no matter how many of the secretive beasts are still out there.

# Red Wolf

CANIS RUFUS

The red wolf (*Canis rufus* or *Canid niger*) is an animal that inspires a great deal of controversy. It did range down through the lower Mississippi Valley and throughout isolated or remote areas of the southeastern United States. There may be some left but what they are now may not be the same species they were or are thought to be.

The destruction of forests, endless hunting and trapping, and poisoning spelled doom for this species from the mid-1800s on. A combination of misinformation and mysticism, among often illiterate people living off the land, made this shy predator into everyman's foe—a supposed killer of livestock and a danger to man. The story of this wolf has always contained so much folklore that a clear picture has been impossible to compile.

First, it was a species apart from the plains wolf, or gray wolf. It was smaller and darker, but otherwise probably quite similar in social and family structure. Where their ranges overlapped, the two species may have interbred. Where trees were cut back and eventually entire forests cut down, conditions better favored the coyote, and that wild canid began its movements into former red-wolf country. The persecution of the red wolf did not stop. Under various guises—self-defense, livestock protection, or predator control, sport hunting and trapping marketable pelts—it went on. There were always reasons why the red wolf should die, but there never really was any sense to any of it.

It is probable that coyotes and red wolves also cross-bred. That was another species added to a probable mix. Dogs, too, when they weren't in packs chasing red wolves, may have bred with them. There have always been plenty of feral dogs in the swamps and woods of the southeast.

Some "supposed" red wolves were held in zoos and still are in collections, but usually no claims are made for their positive identity. The Wild Canid Survival Center near St. Louis has wolves they feel are red wolves, which are generally black, not red. The United States Fish and Wildlife Service has attempted to reintroduce specimens into thick woodlands on barrier islands off North Carolina. Some local residents have expressed their indignation at this threat to their safety and have promised to shoot on sight every wolf they encounter. Fortunately, once the wolves are released from their holding pens into the frequently flooded woodlands, it is unlikely that any resident will ever encounter them, much less be endangered by them.

It is impossible to say if there are any pure red wolves alive on this planet. If they have mixed their genes with gray wolves, coyotes, and feral dogs, in time, the mix would not show as a mix, but the additional genes are there and can never be erased. If there are specimens that have not been hybridized, they are certainly worth saving.

Any animal that can be classified as any kind of wolf in North America and that has survived south of Canada and Alaska should be saved and revered as the ultimate proof of the survival instinct. All wolves, including the little brush wolf called *coyote*, have been assaulted with every possible weapon justified by every imaginable excuse. What we know of the history of the red wolf was the history of the buffalo before it vanished, and is the story of the gray wolf as well. The gray wolf has the advantage of being able to retreat into Canada and thence northward, where there are plenty of prey and few people. The red wolf, on the other hand, was caught in a vise between expanding agriculture and animal husbandry, logging, and the kind of boredom that makes some men want to shoot anything. The Gulf of Mexico and the Atlantic Ocean are at the red wolf's back. It has been subjected to disease in its decreasing range. Mange and heartworm are just two of the problems any canid faces in the areas where red wolves might still be found. And wolves in the wild do not get veterinary care. With its back to the water, has the red wolf been squeezed to death?

# Polar Bear

## THALARCTOS MARITIMUS

One of the most spectacular of the world's carnivores is the huge white polar bear *(Thalarctos maritimus)*, the only member of its genus. It grows to be well over a half a ton, in the range of twelve to thirteen hundred pounds. That makes it second in size only to the great brown bears among all of the terrestrial carnivores that have survived into modern times.

The range of the polar bear is circumpolar, around the top of the world. It does appear in some places south of the Arctic Circle, such as at the southern tip of Hudson Bay in Manitoba. That location, at about 60 degrees north latitude near the town of Churchill, is the southernmost population of the polar bear today.

The polar bear is more nearly a total carnivore than any other member of the bear family (Ursidae). It is poorly conditioned by instinct to hunt on land, although it is likely to kill most other animals that get too near, including other polar bears. Females with cubs keep clear of the boars until the cubs are big enough to get away from a really cranky adult male.

Anything polar bears kill is likely to be eaten on land as well as on the ice. That makes them cannibalistic. They will also eat carrion. They hunt alone after they become adults, but if a whale is beached, or any other large carcass like a walrus encountered, a number of bears may gather for the feast.

Unfortunately, polar bear and human encounters can end very badly for one species or the other. Human beings have often been killed by surprising a polar bear, which is easy to do. They have poor eyesight, but very keen hearing and a sharp sense of smell. On the other side, sportsmen have always rated these white giants as one of the true highlights of a trophy-hunting career. A polar bear hide sells for thousands of dollars. In the past, polar bear rugs constituted a significant trade for native hunters. In the United States, any traffic in polar bear skins is illegal since it is classified as a marine mammal. Until quite recently, though, they were hunted in Alaska.

Polar bears are not, as once thought, an endangered species. The world population of wild bears is difficult to estimate but between twenty and thirty thousand is probably realistic. They were much reduced in numbers in recent times, however. The polar bear is thought to be one of the few species of mammals whose population was seriously impacted by sport hunting. Polar bears are now strictly protected in the Soviet Union with its enormous Arctic coast as well as in the United States, i.e. Alaska. It is unlikely that the polar bear population will shrink again unless climactic changes alter the Arctic or some other factor moves or reduces the bear's natural food—seals, walruses, and whales. They are capable of killing smaller whales such as narwhals and belugas. The polar bear has become a very specialized animal, so much so that when the ice breaks up at the end of June in Hudson Bay, the bears come ashore and fast until the ice forms again at the beginning of November. Unless they come upon some food serendipitously during that long period, they will simply not eat at all.

Polar bears do very well in captivity. Typically thirty or more zoos report births every year, and the species really can be considered self-sustaining. Since polar bears require, and should always have, large display areas—*not* cages—with a pool large enough for swimming, and since they do not do well in groups as adults, the babies born almost always have to be dispersed by sale or trade. Few zoos have enough space and money for more than one polar bear exhibit. There are almost always cubs available for any zoo that can afford to obtain them and exhibit them.

It is questionable whether zoos in very warm climates should have this species at all. Having their own swimming pool does help, certainly, but the bears probably suffer from the heat. Unfortunately, polar bears are extremely dangerous in captivity, as they can be in the wild. Keepers are always on the alert, certain that their charges are just waiting for them to make a mistake. When children or deranged people have crossed safety barriers, there have been very serious accidents and more than a few deaths. Keeping polar bears and people apart is absolutely essential, and some zoos take elaborate precautions with moats, television surveillance, and keepers on the lookout for people foolish enough to attempt to outwit the regular safety devices and systems.

# Beluga Whale

## DELPHINAPTERUS LEUCAS

One of the most commonly encountered whales in captivity is the beluga or white whale *(Delphinapterus leucas)*. It is often referred to as medium-sized, but when compared with such oceanic giants as the blue, finback, humpback, or sperm whale, it is tiny. Just over thirteen feet seems to be about record length, with twelve feet the average. Even the killer whale—actually a porpoise, and another species now often seen in captivity—is commonly twice that length. Big bull orcas are closer to three times larger—up to thirty or even thirty-one feet.

The range of the beluga is normally the coastal Arctic and sometimes down into the rivers of the far north when the ice breaks up for the short summer. It is an animal easily distinguishable and readily spotted from boats or from the air. Its stark white, torpedo-shaped form stands out against the dark waters. Its rounded forehead and total lack of a dorsal fin make identification certain. Nothing else in the sea looks anything like it. That white color doesn't appear until the animal is mature, between its fourth and fifth year. Juveniles are gray, blue-gray, or even blackish before they begin to fade.

Belugas feed on fish, octopus and squid, and crustaceans. They are gregarious and are generally found in groups of from six to twelve animals, and at times in much larger gatherings of up to eighty or more. At certain times of the year, hundreds can be seen along a few miles of coast, often near the mouth of a large river or bay. Whether such associations are breeding congregations or responses to feeding opportunities, or both, remains unclear. Except to their prey, belugas are quiet, peaceful animals quite secretive in their ways. The suggestion that they live in a very harsh environment is relative and a matter of our own projection. The Arctic, even seas and harbors clogged with ice, is not harsh for animals that have evolved to live in that setting. It is their norm. Everything they are and do suits them to it perfectly.

Belugas do, inexplicably, stray. One or two may appear un-expectedly as far south as New York City (around 43 degrees north latitude, the same as Madrid, Spain), but they seldom last long. The number of boats in those waters so far south of the animal's normal range and the racket their engines make are apparently confusing, and the whales seem unable to adapt. They can be quickly run down and killed by the impact, or so severely damaged by propellers that they die of shock and loss of blood.

The life of the beluga at home in the Arctic is not entirely peaceful either. They are hunted by orca, by polar bears when they get too close to ice floes, and by native Americans who use their flesh for themselves and their dogs. There has been some commercial use of their oil and hides.

Because of their relatively remote natural habitat, one would think the beluga out of the reach of man's harm. That is not the case. Pollution is growing even at extremely high latitudes (in addition to far-too-common oil spills). There are depredations by native people, some of whom are legitimately subsistence hunters, and many who are not. These hunters often leave their old skin boats behind and set out in high-speed watercraft, equipped with depth gauges, radios, and powerful outboard motors. They use scope-sighted rifles more often than harpoons, and some even use spotter aircraft. Today, with low-flying, high-winged Cessnas linked by radio to boats with fifty- and sixty-horsepower motors, the beluga is in trouble.

A pattern is evolving in the Arctic that could doom the populations that have used those waters for uncounted millennia. It is extremely unlikely that captive collections would be able to keep the species going for very long. Belugas are too expensive to keep, take up far too much room if they are to be captive bred, and their lifespan away from their native Arctic currents is too brief to allow for general optimism. Human attitudes are going to have to change enough in the years immediately ahead to allow the beluga space and food where it really belongs if the species is to survive.

# Gray Wolf

## CANIS LUPUS

No terrestrial animal on earth except man has had a greater range than the gray wolf *(Canis lupus)*. And no animal on earth has been more persecuted by man. No animal has had more nonsense believed or written about it. There are more legends about wolves than about any animal man has had an opportunity to interact with.

The gray wolf is the largest of all living wild canids. An extremely large male can weigh close to two hundred pounds although the average is well below that, closer to one hundred pounds. These animals both as individuals and subspecies are products of the land they live on and the prey they can take. Given their range, the variability is not difficult to understand. The gray wolf's range is given as all habitats of the Northern Hemisphere except for tropical forests and true deserts. That means it has ranged over most of Eurasia at some time in history. It is still found, of course, in Alaska and Canada, and has been found in Greenland and all of the continental United States except the southeastern corner and much of California, for some reason. It has even been found in Mexico, where some few may still exist. That is a vast area when one considers the width of the Soviet Union plus the rest of Europe including the British Isles and the depth of North America from high in Alaska to deep into Mexico, from the Arctic in Asia to far south into India. All this is evidence of this species' incredible intelligence and endless flexibility.

The prey of these often large and always sociable animals has included just about anything that can be killed, literally anything from moose to mice. Unfortunately, it has also included domestic livestock and that is undoubtedly why the species has been so maligned and so persecuted by man.

One strange aspect of the wolf-man relationship has been the insistence that its natural food includes human beings. There are probably many reasons why this myth has had such universal currency although it has been extremely rare, if ever true. In Turkey and Iran, particularly, the small subspecies *Canis lupus palipes,* a form still found from Israel to India, has been very often infected with rabies. Wolves with rabies almost certainly attacked human beings. Wolves, like most predators, also take carrion since it is safer and far easier to get. In times of war and plague when natural prey may be in short supply and unburied human bodies abound, wolves probably have taken advantage of the situation. Similarly, trappers and other travelers in remote areas that have died of any of a number of causes, including starvation and exposure, may have been fed on by wolves and tracks near a half-eaten body could reinforce the legends about man-eating. The facts? In all of man's long history in North America, there is not a single verifiable account of wolves killing a human being. There have been longstanding rewards for evidence proving otherwise, but they have never been claimed. Wolves have eaten dead human beings but, as far as we know, not live ones.

As a result of the hatred the myths have encouraged, and because wolves have come into conflict with man over stock killing, the wolf has been driven to extinction over much of its former range. That means subspecies we have known about as well as others that went before they were identified. There are no wolves left in the British Isles or Ireland. They are gone from virtually all of western Europe except parts of Scandinavia and Russia proper farther to the east. They have been eliminated in all but a very few pockets in the United States, except Alaska. They survive in the Middle East, but in limited areas. It is the same over all of their range. Traps, guns, poison, aerial assault, reduction in natural prey, all have played their role. The wolf is one of the few animals people have generally considered to be an out-and-out enemy.

Hundreds of wolves are born in zoos every year. Some of them are almost certainly bona fide subspecies, but most are questionable as to origin. Man began keeping wolves long before he began keeping records. As the ancestor of the domestic dog, the wolf can breed with our larger dogs and, indeed, is known to have done so with some regularity. Coyotes, a different species *(Canis latrans)* can also mate with both wolves and dogs, so hybridization in the wild has also been a problem. Because of a recent consciousness of the wolf's true role and general innocence of the many crimes with which it has been charged, the species may fare better than in the past. Still, the world will probably remain a relatively inhospitable place for animals as powerful and as thoroughly wonderful as the gray wolf.

# Mountain Tapir

## TAPIRUS PINCHAGUE

There is no doubt that the four species of tapirs left in the world (Baird's, Mountain, and the Brazilian, all from Latin America; and the Malayan, from Burma and Sumatra) are remnants of a much larger group of odd-toed ungulates (Perissodactyla) that once ranged over a much larger portion of the earth including Borneo, North America, and China. All four surviving species are now considered endangered. They parallel the other perissodactyls, the equines, with only one species of wild horse left, and the once widespread rhinoceroses, with only five species still alive. It has been a hard-luck group of animals that appears to be ending its tenure on earth. This tragedy could be averted if human beings, the source of all misery, really cared. If all the wild species go, only the wild horse will have left a legacy, the domestic horse, which is descended from it.

The mountain tapir (*Tapirus pinchague,* according to some authorities, or *Tapirus roulini,* according to others) is a perfect example of a peaceful, solitary animal that cannot hold its own against the onslaught man has mounted against it. It is hunted as food by some Indian tribes in its range, although there are Indian tribes that don't hunt the tapir, for religious reasons. The tapir's range is limited to small areas in the high Colombian Cordilleras and the wildest regions of the equatorial Andes. That takes it into pockets in Venezuela, Ecuador, and Peru. There are few if any corridors between these pockets of survivors, and the species' range is apparently being chopped into increasingly smaller areas. The tapir does not fare well when man is around.

The mountain tapir is in many ways a very intolerant or at least inflexible animal and therein lies the biggest problem. It is seldom if ever reported below 7,500 feet on its favored mountain slopes. Its tracks have been found much higher up, between thirteen and fourteen thousand feet in areas of permanent snow. It must have areas with stunted trees and shrubs, vegetation that has been dwarfed by low temperatures and exposure to winds. The mental image of the tapir in the steaming tropical lowland forest does not apply to this species.

The chaparrales where the mountain tapir roams and leaves its distinct trails that have apparently been in use for centuries is an area now being assaulted by ever-growing herds of cattle. When livestock and their human attendants move into an area, the intolerant tapirs move out. They simply abandon yet another stronghold and become even more confined than before. They insist on their solitude. They are what German scientists refer to as "culture-fleers." That has probably always been the way with all tapir species, the four that survive and probably very many more that are gone.

The mountain tapir (it is also called the woolly tapir) is a rare animal in captivity as well as in the wild. It has been bred in zoos but not often, nowhere near enough to be encouraging. There are a great many Malayan tapirs in zoos, a couple of hundred, at least, and a fair number have been successfully bred. There are a few Baird's tapirs in zoos, as well, but they are not good captive breeders either.

The perissodactyls, especially the rhinoceroses and tapirs, can be placed back in the wild, unlike the large predators, when and if preserves can be established and secured in their natural habitat. They probably would not do too well as transplants in different habitats. The captive propagation of these species is absolutely essential to their future. It appears that of all of them, the rhinoceroses and tapirs, with the probable exception of the white rhinoceros in southern Africa, will succumb to the activities of man before secure preserves of sufficient size can be established and the wild stocks given time to rebuild and spread out. With these species, time is rapidly running out, and the role of captive collections is absolutely necessary for their survival.

# Margay

## FELIS WIEDI

In all of the world, there are only thirty-seven species of wild cats left (plus some subspecies, it seems certain) although there were once very many more. Twenty-eight of the smaller cats, which are most of the existing wild cats belong to the genus *Felis*. There are only four genera left. Each species is a magnificent remnant of some of the greatest hunters ever evolved in the animal kingdom.

The smaller cats in the genus *Felis* come from Africa, Asia, Europe, and North and South America as well as the Middle East and a number of islands in different parts of the world. Even the domestic house cat belongs to this group that includes bobcats, lynx, jungle cats, pampas cats, desert cats, the ocelot, margay, cougar, serval, and jaguarundi. It is a mixed bag of the beautiful and, unfortunately often, the rare.

It is very difficult to be definitive when writing about these cats because science is anything but secure in the present breakdown of species and even genera. No doubt there will be refinements made as long as there are cats to worry about. In the words of science, the cats' "classification is very unstable."

Scientific niceties aside, the cats of the world are in trouble in the wild. They tend to be secretive, with the obvious exception of the lion and one or two other species such as the cheetah. They need prey to hunt and the room to take their prey. There is a fallacy that is almost impossible to shake loose that predators control the populations of their prey. It is the other way around. The prey dictate the population of the predators. When prey is hard to find, the cats reduce or stop their breeding activity. They have smaller litters more widely spaced, and when things get really bad, they abandon or kill their young. It is far more important in nature that proven breeders survive, than untried cubs. Among lions, for example, males will eat their young or at least crowd them away from a kill when food is scarce. It may seem harsh, but survival of species is what is paramount in nature, not the safety of cubs with cute faces.

So there is the problem of sufficient prey. A second desperate need of many of the smaller cats is not to be hunted or trapped for their splendid coats. For years, the mindless fur industry paid high prices for cat skins, and a number of the handsomely marked cats were placed in serious jeopardy be-cause of their beauty. It is becoming illegal in more and more countries to import or export cat skins, and the industry will apparently dry up in time.

Many of the smaller cats, perhaps most of them, require forested areas because of their secretive, often nocturnal life-styles. One of these is the splendid, patterned margay *(Felis wiedi)*. Under normal conditions, long since made impossible, this essentially forest cat ranged from northern Mexico to northern Argentina and did in fact appear, although rarely, in the Texas border country. In Mexico and Central America, margays were taken for their pelts and for the pet trade, although few of them survived capture, transport, mishandling in pet shops, and then apartment life.

Because of predation by man and because of that endless conservation nightmare, deforestation, the margay is gone from much of its original range and may be in serious trouble in many other. At best, its range can be described as discontinuous. A number of zoos, perhaps as many as ten or twelve, have managed to breed margays every year, and there are a fair number in captivity. It is unlikely that they will be bred in very large numbers in the immediate future because, unless given very handsome and extremely well designed enclosures, they are among the less spectacular zoo exhibits. That goes for most of the smaller cats. They are a kind of sidebar to the lions, tigers, leopards, snow leopards, and cheetah. In zoos as well as in the wild, these small, shy animals are easily overlooked. There is the problem, too, that captive populations of the smaller cats (as is the case with the great cats of *Panthera*) will do wild populations little good. Despite all the good intentions and deep devotion of George and Joy Adamson with their beloved Elsa in the saga *Born Free* no one really knows a practical way to reestablish wild, self-sustaining feline populations from stock that is captive bred for generations.

Whether it is the lynx in Canada, the bobcat in the United States, the margay in Central and South America, the serval and caracal in Africa, and any or all of the others, some accommodations are going to have to be made to leave enough habitat intact, or the world's smaller cats will simply vanish. The fur and pet trades will have to be totally banned as far as these feline species are concerned.

# Giant Anteater

## MYRMECOPHAGA TRIDACTYLA

The order Edentata consists of approximately thirty rather primitive animals, the tropical American anteaters and sloths, and the tropical-through-temperate-zone armadillos. The Latin word *endentata* means "no teeth" although only in the case of the anteaters is this true. The order has apparently always been restricted to the New World, arising in the tropical zone about sixty million years ago.

There are seventeen genera today, although there have apparently been at least 175 at various times. The order has been shrinking for millions of years. Starting out in topical climates the edentates slowly worked their way north and eventually gave rise to the incredibly massive giant armadillos famous from the La Brea Tar Pit finds in the Los Angeles basin. All that is left of this primitive order in the United States today is the small nine-banded armadillo of several southern-tier states.

In this order is the family Myrmecophagidae with its single species, the giant anteater. The giant anteater *(Myrmecophaga tridactyla)* is one of the most bizarre-looking of the entire order. It is also the largest in modern times. It grows to be up to nearly forty inches long and over eighty-five pounds in weight. Unlike its smaller cousins, it does not climb trees nor does it burrow. It is active during the day in areas that are not heavily populated with people, but will switch to mainly nighttime wandering and feeding when there are many people around. When it is time to sleep, it curls up in as private a spot as it can find, puts its immensely long nose between its forelegs, and covers it all with a shroud formed by its long and bushy tail.

The giant, despite its large size, lives strictly on ants, termites, some beetle grubs, and possibly, on occasion, some fruit. In pursuit of its principal prey, it uses its very long and powerful front nails to rip into nests. Then it swoops up everything it can reach with its long and extendable tongue, made sticky with a heavy coating of saliva. That tongue can extend as much as two feet although it is only about half an inch wide at its base. It is a highly specialized feeding instrument. It has been suggested that a single giant anteater consumes thirty thousand ants and termites in one day. Its influence on the insect community may not be as profound as that figure might sound. The number of ants and termites in a single acre of tropical forest or savanna can amount to billions. Ants and termites, in fact, represent a significant percentage of the biomass of a tropical forest community. In an undisturbed area, the giant anteater is not likely ever to use up its food supply.

The range given for the giant anteater extends from the southern zones of Belize in Central America to the northern part of Argentina. That would take it through the entire Amazon Basin. The anteater is an efficient swimmer and is undeterred by rivers unless preyed upon by anaconda, caiman, or piranha.

There are giant anteaters in captivity, where they constitute an interesting display with their bizarre size and shape and their long cylindrical snouts. An egg, milk, fruit, meal worm, and hamburger diet has been evolved by zoos and does very well in satisfying the animals needs. They have bred in captivity, and there doesn't seem to be much doubt that there is enough expertise available to step up efforts for increased propagation if that becomes important. That could well happen before long, since the species is already listed as *vulnerable,* a step below *threatened* and two below *endangered.* Although the species does have a very large range historically, there is almost no part of it that is not now suffering from deforestation and land clearing. In areas where that kind of activity has been moving forward most rapidly, the anteaters have been much reduced in number. It is an animal that bears watching, in and out of the zoo.

# Maned Wolf

## CHRYSOCYON BRACHYURUS

The maned wolf of South America *(Chrysocyon brachyurus)* is the largest of all of that vast continent's canines. It is also one of the most difficult to see. It lives on the open grasslands and in the scrub forests in northeastern and southern Brazil, on the pampas of Peru and Paraguay. Because of deforestation, it may be spreading its range into Colombia. It was once found in Uruguay and south of the La Plata River in Argentina but is now almost certainly gone from those areas. It is not really clear why that happened, but more than likely, it was a number of factors combined.

This slender but still substantial animal can weigh as much as fifty pounds despite its very leggy look. Its foxlike head and golden-red color are most unwolflike. Its mane, which it can erect when disturbed or intensely interested in something, is black.

The maned wolf tends to be nocturnal but may also be active at dawn and dusk, activity periods referred to as crepuscular. That is particularly true of the male wolves. They do hunt small animals, but eat far more vegetable matter than the wolves we are more familiar with in the northern hemisphere. They are especially fond of fruit with their tastes varying, of course, according to season and availability.

The maned wolf, with their peculiar open-land gait, does well in captivity, especially when given large spaces to move around in. They do better housed as pairs of the opposite sex rather than males with males or females with females. During the breeding season, they need privacy and a diet high in protein but low in fat. There are usually anywhere between one and two hundred maned wolves in captivity at any one time in thirty-five or more collections. They can be bred in captivity but a zoo has to be willing to devote space and money to the project in order to be successful. Breeding them is seldom a casual or gratuitous occurrence.

Good veterinary supervision is mandatory since maned wolves are subjected to a number of canine diseases and parasites. Cub mortality can be high. No holding of maned wolves will flourish without good observation of behavioral changes and frequent monitoring of droppings.

Although it is unusual in this world, the human inhabitants in the maned wolf's range are relatively indifferent to the animal. An occasional duck, goose, or chicken may be taken, something that does not endear any animal to a farmer, but there is really very little conflict. The kind of hatred leveled at other forms of wolf is not recorded in South America. The wolves do their best not to be seen, and farmers and husbandrymen ignore their presence for the most part. Man and maned wolf are literally species that pass in the night.

There is good reason for more zoos to be breeding this unusual canid than are now doing it, however. Brazil lists the species as endangered. The world arbiters, the IUCN, lists them as vulnerable. That vulnerability is based on the fact that while deforestation has meant the maned wolf can spread out, it is not moving into stable areas like the original pampas. Man is making alterations that can impact food sources, and erosion can eliminate den sites. The maned wolf is adaptable and can utilize a variety of foods now generally available. But that may not always be the case.

Heavy grazing by very large herds of livestock that are required by a burgeoning human population could alter habitat and these strange long-legged canids are not adaptable without limit. No one can know where the break point might come and the populations of these animals plummet. They have been studied in the wild, many of their needs and even preferences are known, but not everything about them is a matter of record. There are too many changes occurring in South America, too many enormous alterations of the open lands and adjacent forests to be casual about any species. The maned wolf is a canine, but a very different kind from the other species we know so much better. Their preservation is a scientific as well as an ethical imperative, and the role of the zoos as species holding facilities is clear. Fortunately, there is no great mystery in how to go about propagating maned wolves. It is a matter of will, space, time, and money. Zoos always must make choices as to the species that will get their attention and therefore their budget. Hopefully, more zoos will decide to place the maned wolf high on their priority list.

# Spectacled Bear

## TREMARCTOS ORNATUS

The spectacled bear *(Tremarctos ornatus)* was once native to the forested slopes of the Andes in Venezuela, Colombia, Ecuador, Bolivia, and Peru. That was a century or more ago. It was frequently found in open clearings as well as in thick forests up to ten thousand feet, and sometimes even considerably higher than that. Like most bears, it adapted to whatever food resources were available each season. It is the only member of the bear family, Ursidae, in all of South America. Compared to the larger brown bears, including the grizzlies, of North America, it is a small animal. It is also retiring. Encounters are by chance or occasionally because of the curiosity that is a hallmark of all bears.

It has been suggested that the spectacled bear is more of a vegetarian than most of the other bears. All bears are really omnivores, although they are members of the order Carnivora. The polar bear is amost wholly a meat eater, and the spectacled bear may be at almost the other end of the spectrum. Still, any bear will take carrion, including livestock found dead or dying from accident or natural causes, and the spectacled bear is no exception. Its unmistakable pugmarks near a dead sheep, pig, horse, or llama would go far to enhance its reputation as a stock killer. The same is true of all bears around the world. Like all the others, the spectacled bear can be aggressive in a chance encounter, and undoubtedly attacks on humans have occurred. However exceptional these attacks may have been, they have underscored man's natural prejudices against this carnivorous species.

There is no doubt that the spectacled bear is now threatened with extinction. Many of the isolated pockets where it is still to be found are so far removed from any controlling agency that local inhabitants can hunt it at will. There are still foreign trophy hunters discovering what is left of South and Central American wildlife. There is deforestation, the use of ever higher and more remote slopes for agriculture and stock grazing. Almost any husbandryman in the world will shoot any bear he sees. Dogs are inveterate enemies of bears although they shared a common ancestor about sixty million years ago. They will chase them, sometimes separating cubs from their mothers. That often spells death for the cubs either because the dogs get to them or because they become hopelessly lost and starve. Partially grown animals seldom know enough about survival skills in a hostile world to make it, and reports of attacks on man or livestock generally involve immature animals. Local people do not take that into account and will still molest and kill females with cubs, leaving the cubs to become nuisances and then be hunted down themselves.

At the northern end of the bear's range, in Venezuela, it was probably always sparsely distributed, and, although there are laws protecting it or at least limiting the take by hunters, the laws are all but unenforceable. Fortunately, there are generally between eighty and a hundred specimens of this species in thirty-five to fifty collections worldwide. They breed well enough in captivity. Any concentration of funds and space allotted to the species would increase the number of viable cubs produced and keep the species going. It may be a very long time, however, before the continent of South America is stable enough and poverty well enough controlled (i.e., reduced) to allow even a potentially carnivorous animal safe haven on native ground. In the meantime, habitat destruction and hunting will continue to limit the population and eventually reduce it to the point of extinction. Then, when males can no longer locate mates, and vice versa, it will be all over *except* for zoos.

# Trumpeter Swan

## CYGNUS CYGNUS BUCCINATOR

The world's largest swan, the trumpeter *(Cygnus cygnus buccinator)*, is a subspecies of the whooper swan. Once, apparently a very long time ago, it ranged south all the way to the lower Mississippi Valley, Maryland, and Florida. Remains have been found in all three areas. More recently the giant ranged into California, Minnesota, Indiana, Iowa, Nebraska, Missouri, Illinois, Louisiana, and probably Texas. Now, the pressures of agriculture, hunting, and adulterated water supplies have forced it north. The natural range that has been left to it is pretty well restricted to Montana, Wyoming, Western Canada (British Columbia and Alberta), and at least the southern part of Alaska.

Reintroduced swans in Minnesota were doing quite well until a season of low rain caused severe water-level drops in the lakes where the birds had been introduced. Those drops exposed lead shot from more than a century and a half of hunting. The swans ingested the shot, and many died from paralyzed digestive systems. They simply starved to death or died of dehydration and pneumonia. It has not put an end to the costly reintroduction enterprise, but it was a very bad setback.

Swans, to nonhunting people, are decorative and indeed symbols of grace, purity, and beauty. To hunters, they are meat and are reportedly good eating, as good as geese. Ever since Europeans arrived on this continent, there has been pressure on native swans and not very much sentimentality. The swans retreated as more and more of their range greeted them with veritable sheets of lead shot coming up at them from boats, blinds, and bushes. Not very long ago, swans appeared in the marketplace and on restaurant menus. There was also a large trade in their skins for the manufacture of powder puffs. They are generally low fliers and come within easy range of gunners lying in wait. The trumpeter never seems to have preferred ocean water and only occasionally reached the shore in its wandering. These are animals of inland waterways, and much of their original range is now inhabited and used by man.

Despite its apparently large original range, the trumpeter is not the really spectacular migrator the other northern white swans are. The whooper, whistler, Jankowski's, and Bewick swans always nested farther north and wintered farther south. The more sedentary trumpeter, weighing up to forty-five pounds, is a much heavier bird than the rest. It wanders just far enough to find open water and food. In that, is resembles the mute swan that was brought here from Europe and has so successfully established itself.

Swans are extremely easy for aviculturists to propagate. They are cooperative as long as they are allowed reasonable room when they have eggs in the nest and young in tow in the water. Both parents are extremely protective, and the male, called a *cob*, can be downright ferocious. That factor does limit the number of swans any zoo can manage at any one time. Private collectors with licenses for protected species breed them, as do various state fish and wildlife authorities. There has been some recovery in the wild population. Reintroduction is bound to work in areas where they have been hunted or driven out in recent times. They are now a protected species and sportsmen seem to be showing more concern than they have in the past. There can be no doubt, however, that some are shot each year. That will probably always be the case, as long as wildfowl hunting is a sport in North America. The way wildfowl numbers have been falling, that pastime might be doomed before too many decades have gone by.

The experts charged with the propagation of these great swans regularly remove eggs from the nest (at some risk to life and limb) shortly after laying has been completed and place them in an incubator. The paired swans then lay a second clutch (this is called *double-clutching*) and more young than normal can be extracted each year.

The trumpeter swan, whose resounding voice has to be heard to be believed, is undoubtedly here to stay. In that fact can be found the attentive hand of man. Some men destroy and despoil, others encourage and protect. The balance seems to be shifting toward the positive side ever so slowly but apparently surely.

# Whooping Crane

## GRUS AMERICANA

The saga of the whooping crane *(Grus americana)* is an international success story—a symbol of wildlife conservation at its best. For once, science, law, bureaucracy, and goodwill have coupled with comon sense to save one of the most magnificent and seriously endangered of all animal species in the Western Hemisphere. As recently as 1941, there were no more than fourteen of these birds known to be surviving in the wild.

Traditionally, whooping cranes had wintered along the coast of the Gulf of Mexico from Florida to Texas, particularly near Aransas, Texas, and then as now they bred in the Mackenzie District in Canada and northward along the Mackenzie River. Whooping cranes require three things besides food to survive: quiet, isolated marshes in the north for their nests, safe passage to and from the southern ends of their migratory routes, and safety in the south while they wait for the weather to break and allow them to return north to their marshes in the spring.

What happened to the large flocks appears to be clear. They were shot during their migrations. It was as simple as that. The National Audubon Society went all out with an educational campaign. Canada undertook the birds' protection in the north and the United States in the south, and that dual protection was implacably enforced.

Concurrently, a campaign to proliferate the species got under way. Since whoopers produce two eggs but rarely raise more than one, young ornithologists made the exhausting trek into the cranes' mosquito-ridden northern marshes and removed one egg from each nest they could reach. The eggs were carried south and some were put on the nests of the related sandhill cranes. By that time, their population decimated by hunters, whoopers were wintering only at Aransas, on the Texas coast north of Corpus Christi. Whooping-crane chicks that were hatched from eggs put with the sandhills migrated with their surrogate parents to Louisiana. No longer was the entire remaining whooping-crane population in a position where a single storm could destroy them all.

Other eggs were taken to the U.S. Fish and Wildlife Service's facility for endangered species propagation at Patuxent, Maryland, and were hatched there. In time a good captive breeding nucleus was established. It has since been split with other captive-bred birds going to the International Crane Foundation in Baraboo, Wisconsin, where Dr. George Archibald has done such a splendid job with all the endangered crane species.

By 1959, eighteen years after the low point of fourteen birds, there were thirty-three whoopers at Aransas, and by 1968, there were fifty. Slowly the number in the wild increased until today it is well over a hundred and climbing in Aransas alone, with others in Louisiana as part of the sandhill population. And with Patuxent having demonstrated how readily the birds breed in captivity, it is certain that captive-bred birds released into a wintering wild population will migrate with them, signaling each other during their marathon flights with the incredible call that gave the whooper its name.

The enforcement of the protective laws in the United States and Canada will probably have to be strictly enforced forever, and the whoopers' protected breeding grounds in Canada may well have to be further extended, while the steps taken to expand and disperse the captive population will have to continue. Whoopers can be seen in the wild as they rest during migration on the Platte River in Nebraska, or at Aransas where most bird-watchers hope to make a pilgrimage one day. Meanwhle, the captive birds, fully protected and breeding, constitute a necessary and comforting reserve. No one really know how many whooping cranes there should be in the wild, but it is unlikely there will ever again be as many as there once were. As for the hunters who still illegally kill a few birds every year during their migration, the law will have to remain as tough as ever. It can never be too tough.

# California Condor

## GYMNOGYPS CALIFORNIANUS

In all of the world of zoos and wildlife conservation, there is no clearer, simpler, or more perilous situation than that of the California condor *(Gymnogyps californianus)*. The species is extinct in the wild, and all that survive are twenty-odd animals living in two zoos, in Los Angeles and San Diego. Thus the fate of one of the only two condor species left in the world (the other is the Andean condor *(Vultur gryphus)* is now in the hands of a few dedicated men and women. If the species' perpetuation does not work out in those two southern California zoos, there are no more reserves. With less than thirty specimens remaining, the California condor is one of the rarest life-forms on earth.

Back in 1827, the condor was found all the way north to Fort Vancouver, Washington, down through Oregon, and south to Baja, California. And there are very old bones in museum collections, found in caves in Nevada, new Mexico, and Texas, incidating that in prehistoric times the species may have ranged all the way to Florida. Yet as a cliff nester it must have had very different habits back then. Recent birds have not been nest builders but rather have laid their single eggs among pebbles to keep them from rolling out of the high caves where they hatched their young. There are no cliffs along the Gulf of Mexico—none, certainly, in Florida.

The population of condors was decreasing steadily from well before the turn of the century. At that time, when egg collecting was a widespread (and destructive) hobby, a condor egg sold for $300. With a working man then earning $12 for a six-day week, you have some indication of the rarity of the bird even a hundred years ago.

The single egg produced by the condor, unfortunately, is laid every *other* year, giving the species one of the lowest re-productive rates of any surviving species of bird. So when the last condor in the wild was trapped a couple of years ago (after longtime political infighting as well as genuine scientific disagreement), the die was cast. At that time there were no more than a half-dozen captive breeding pairs. In their natural state, the birds had originally fed on dead wildlife, and when man replaced the wildlife in their habitats with livestock, they fed on dead sheep, cows, and horses. But then, as veterinary medicine began its accelerating climb to its present state of excellence, there were fewer and fewer dead animals of any kind for the strictly carrion-eating bird to feed on. So that is another factor in the condor's demise.

It is hoped that with careful management, the first egg a pair of captive condors produces can be removed and artificially incubated. That should encourage the birds to "double-clutch"—that is, produce a second egg. Then, when the numbers have (one hopes) been built up, it will be time to decide when and where they may be released back into the wild. Their last known range north of Los Angeles didn't do a very good job of supporting them in their last years as a free-living species. Now, no one can be sure if they ever will live there again. And if not there, where?

The wild-living condor is a relatively shy animal around its nest, and while it may be curious about people at other times, and even circle overhead to investigate their activities, it is all too likely to abandon its previous chick or egg if people come too close. So wherever the condor is released, if it ever will be, it will have to have privacy. That means no construction, and no oil or mineral exploration and exploitation—a difficult world to reconstruct in California even for the sake of the bird that bears the state's name.

# Thick-Billed Parrot

## RHYNCHOPSITTA PACHYRHYNCHA

The thick-billed parrot *(Rhynchopsitta pachyrhyncha)* is today a relatively rare bird of the highland pine forests of the Mexican plateau, a creature of the Sierra Madre. There are probably two subspecies. As recently as the early 1920s, the parrots were occasionally seen in southern Arizona and New Mexico.

Their breeding range was undoubtedly always on the high plateau but in the nonbreeding season they did wander over the lowlands. It was then they wandered north into the American Southwest.

It is not known for certain just what happened to the thick-billed parrot (its name is deserved: its bill is very heavy for a rather small bird) but all indications are the villain was the same old one, rapid increase in human population and ever greater demands on the land. When the human assault really gets under way in an area, the trees are the first things to go. They provide building material, firewood, and clear land for pasturage and general agriculture. Trees also provide nesting sites and material, food and cover for birds. If birds have evolved to use big trees, and the big trees are taken, the birds are lost. In a very real sense, their world crumbles. The cutting of the big trees on the high Mexican plateau spelled doom for the large Mexican woodpeckers and nearly did the same for these handsome parrots, one of the relatively few psittacine birds native to North America.

There are generally thick-billed parrots in about twenty-five zoos worldwide and they number a hundred or more. Those shown here are in Los Angeles. A very few zoos have bred them, and experience with the species has been increasing. There is the not unrealistic hope that specimens may eventually be released into the wild to again wander some of the areas along the Mexican border where they were seen until shortly after World War I.

Deforestation was the principal villain in the piece, but undoubtedly there was some persecution as well for pets, for plumage, and just for target practice. In areas where the bird has traditionally been found, concern for wildlife has not been the major preoccupation of the local inhabitants. It is not the best place, in fact, to be a nonhuman member of the animal kingdom, domestic or wild.

It is an unfortunate fact of the wildlife conservation ethic that there is usually some degree of sentimentality that is part of the effort or at least precedes it. That emotional investment is noticeably lacking in many parts of the world including, it should be quickly noted, parts of the United States. It can be extremely difficult to get a plant or animal conservation scheme into gear when it runs against the grain of the people who are needed not only to cooperate but pitch in and help. In any area, there may be a few local conservationists who are the very best conservationists of all; but they can't function effectively in a vacuum. A remote Mexican highland where good money can be had for timber, or for even working to cut and transport someone else's timber, is not the best place to be a parrot, rare or not. It is the same all over the world. Except in rare instances local fauna loses its charm and fascination before the local people are half grown. The rest of the people in the world may have trouble understanding that factor, but before condemning the attitudes of others, they should check and see how they are treating their own fauna and flora.

The thick-billed parrot may be able to make a comeback if existing wild stock is left in peace and augmented with animals from captivity, but only if some of the Sierra Madre's forests are allowed to stand unmolested. If the trees are there and the parrots are protected, the situation could turn around. It would certainly be a high point for the conservation of North American wildlife if the thick-billed again wandered north into New Mexico and Arizona with any degree of regularity. The bird-watchers would come from around the world to share in the spectacle.

# Laysan Duck

## ANAS PLATYRHYNCHOS LAYSANENSIS

The Laysan duck, also frequently referred to as the Laysan teal, is an inhabitant of one of the Hawaiian Archipelago's western-most outposts. The island Laysan is uninhabited except for visiting scientists. A permit is required to even land there.

The rare teal, which wasn't discovered until 1828, was once found on both Laysan and Lisianski islands. It has now vanished from any former habitat, known or unknown, except Laysan. Its recovery there has been slow and at times problematical. Since its range is so very limited—the island has a total area of 1,020 acres—and the teal can only use a relatively small part of that, the lagoons, tidal pools, and marshes, it will always be a rare bird in the wild.

The real problem started in 1890 when rabbits were purposefully introduced to the island. The foreign mammals reproduced rapidly. The ground cover began to vanish, gobbled up by the tide of hungry lagomorphs. With that alteration of habitat, erosion by wind and rain was inevitable, and the insect-eating Laysan duck began to disappear along with another bird, the Laysan finch. Both barely survived and are still listed as endangered. Less fortunate were the Laysan millerbird, rail, and honeycreeper. All three were wiped out.

It was evident what the unwise introduction of an exotic mammal had done, and in 1923, the rabbits were eliminated. The plant life began to recover, but it was almost too late. Between 1910 and 1920, the total population had fallen to just twenty birds. By 1989, with the vegetation restored, the population had climbed to five hundred. It may still go up somewhat from there.

Late in the 1950s, captive propagation was deemed necessary. The wild population was just too vulnerable on so small an island. One major oceanic storm or tidal wave could wipe them all out, as could disease in so confined an area. Specimens were trapped and dispersed for captive breeding to the New York Zoological Society (Bronx Zoo) and other zoos including San Diego, England's Wildfowl Trust on the Severn estuary, San Antonio, and some outstanding private collections. Zoos and breeding farms around the world now raise the Laysan duck or teal. There are regular bird-exchange programs to avoid any more inbreeding than is unavoidable. There is the problem that every specimen alive today in captivity and back on the species' native island is descended from the twenty birds that survived after about 1910.

It is not at all unusual for twenty to thirty zoological collections to report successful hatching and rearing of the Laysan teal today. The population is building on Laysan. That population can be augmented at any time from captive stock. It is safe to say that the Laysan teal has been successfully plucked back from the very edge of oblivion. It could have easily followed those three other Laysan species that succumbed to the appetite of the unwanted and unneeded rabbits. They didn't harm the birds directly, but they did destroy their habitat, at least temporarily. In nature that is the greatest insult of all.

The saving of the Laysan duck from extinction is a letter-perfect story of how conscientious scientists and government, along with zoos, can swing into action. Field biologists must determine the nature of the problem and the extent of the damage. When that is clear, a program has to be agreed upon and then implemented. First, rabbits had to go. Then the existing ducks had to be protected against unnecessary intrusion. When the population could tolerate the risk, some specimens had to be removed and placed in just the right captive collections where propagation was all but guaranteed. The captive stock and the remaining wild birds had to be monitored, with both situations governed by whatever means necessary to keep both arms of the effort moving forward. The result is that a species, unique to a very small area of the world that surely will be needed for study by future generations of ornithologists, did not become extinct despite its terrible plunge in that direction. Even with vanishing wildlife, there can be success stories.

# Nene

## BRANTA SANDVICENSIS

The theory goes that ten thousand years ago, or even farther back than that, a flock of Canada geese were caught by a bad storm while migrating along the west coast of what one day would be called the United States. The winds were apparently so strong that they blew the geese far out to sea. Many of the geese, no doubt, were lost, but some managed to survive and continue westward in their disrupted and disoriented migration. They finally landed on inland ponds or in sheltered bays of what would eventually be called the Sandwich Islands, and still later Hawaii.

In isolation, the Canada geese continued to breed. If any did attempt to migrate after that, they were almost certainly lost at sea. Without the weather signals they had had as warnings in North America that migration time had arrived, enough of the geese apparently stayed in place and began evolving into a totally new species. In time, it became the bird we now know as the Hawaiian goose or nene *(Branta sandvicensis)*. Its close affinity to the ancestral Canada goose is apparent to ornithologists, but the new species looks very different and is one of the most handsome of all geese.

That history is a theory, conjecture really, but it seems to be the most likely scenario. Ornithologists have put the nene in *Branta*, the same genus as the several forms of Canada goose.

In modern times, when fauna began being observed and recorded, the nene was reported from only two islands in the archipelago, Hawaii and Maui. Whether in fact it ever occurred on other islands in the group is not known.

In the nineteenth century, there were estimated to be about 25,000 nene on the two islands, but human predation was severe, and the two populations began diminishing rapidly. Rats no doubt came ashore from whaling ships. It is quite possible that the whalers put pigs ashore so that they could hunt fresh meat whenever they passed that way. Pigs, dogs, and cats were introduced to both islands by settlers. The nene, a ground nester like its probable ancestor, had its nests destroyed and its eggs crushed by rooting feral hogs. Its young were attacked by rats, cats, and dogs. Those that did grow to maturity faced hunters with shotguns, hunters who had no legal restraints. The nene did not stand a chance.

By 1948, the nene was gone from Maui. On Hawaii, the largest island in the archipelago that bears its name, there were perhaps fifty birds left. Certain that it was the only thing they could do to head off the impending extinction of the nene, concerned scientists trapped all the geese they could find and put them into three widely separated captive breeding programs: Litchfield, Connecticut; Pohakuloa Game Farm, Hawaii; and Sir Peter Scott's Wildfowl Trust at Slimbridge on the Severn Estuary in southern England.

The geese did very well in captivity, as was to be expected, so well that between 1960 and 1964, 150 of the captive-bred and -hatched nene were reintroduced into safe areas in Hawaii, both on the big island itself and in Haleakala Crater on Maui, where they were known to have been before the big decline in the nineteenth century. The populations on the two islands have grown through the years, and there are now hundreds, where once there were very nearly none.

Breeding nuclei were also shipped to zoos and private collections that were being operated on a professional basis. This was done so that a freak weather occurrence or an outbreak of disease could not seriously endanger the species. Zoos all over the United States, Canada, and Europe now have young nene hatch every year. It is clear that between a growing wild population and a widely dispersed and well-managed captive breeding program, the species is safe again. It was all done with fewer than fifty birds, the last fifty of their kind on earth.

The story of the Hawaiian goose parallels the stories of the American and European bison and several others that appear in this book. It is a success story that operates on the principle that there are times and places where wild animals can only survive if they are taken from the wild, removed from harm's way, and put into protective custody where careful curatorship becomes stewardship and gives the species a second chance. The Mongolian wild horse, the only truly wild horse left in the world, and Père David's deer are two more species that exist only because of captive breeding. Time ran out for them in the wild. It is hoped that the same thing can be done for the California condor and a long list of other species as well. The story of the nene gives courage to conservationists, who might otehrwise be meek when it came to eliminating a wild species in the wild. It certainly isn't the most desirable route to follow, but when there is no alternative but extinction, it is clearly time to act.

# Harpy Eagle

## HARPIA HARPYJA

An eagle of tropical American rain forests, the mighty harpy eagle *(Harpia harpyja)*, the only species in its genus, is not the high-soaring bird that other eagles inevitably are. It hunts and nests among tall trees, often up to two hundred feet above the forest floor, where it preys on monkeys, particularly capuchin monkeys, sloths, agouti, porcupine, coatimundi, and opossum. It also hunts macaws and parrots, although that is not known for certain.

The great eagle nests so high up, and its plumage blends in so well with the tall silk-cotton and mahogany trees it favors, that studies of its behavior have been sporadic and not always very systematic and informative. Often the only way it can be known that a harpy eagle is in an area is by a pile of bones at the foot of a tree. In size and habit, this species is apparently closer to the Philippine monkey-eating eagle than any other bird, bearing that proudest and most awe-inspiring of all avian names, eagle. Of all the eagles, the harpy may be the most powerful, with a head-to-tail length of up to three feet. As is usual with birds of prey, the females are characteristically larger than the males.

Although its range of Central and northern South America is vast, it is assumed that harpy eagles are not very common. Their food demands are high, so their individual territories are probably large. Nests may be ten or more miles apart. Despite their great size, their very broad wings make them swift and agile, deadly hunters among the trees they inhabit. They swoop up from below to reach their nests or to grab a monkey or sloth off a tree. Animals conditioned to the presence of the harpy eagle in their habitat shrink from any hint of a shadow, as well they might. The feet and talons of the great hunter are huge. Once they have rolled shut, nothing the hunter has chosen to grab can squirm or shake itself loose.

Twenty or more zoos are likely to have harpy eagles on display at any one time. They do breed in captivity, although not in great numbers. It is possible the normal reproductive rhythm would produce no more than one egg every other year. The young are dependent on their parents for food for an extended period of time. Full maturity probably does not occur until the eagle is somewhere between four and five years old.

It is not clear exactly what factors have played the largest role in making the harpy eagle relatively uncommon. It is obviously a slow reproducer, it does require a large territorial block for every nest, and the young do occupy the adults for a protracted period. Where there is deforestation, of course, the species is doomed. When the big trees are gone, so are prey and nesting sites.

With their rather unpleasant habit of killing monkeys—something man has not hesitated to do with far less reason, however—and very valuable macaws, some of which can bring as much as $7,000 on the retail market, the harpy eagle, never a bird well known to many people, is unlikely to get much sympathy from people in their normal range. Reproduction is so slow that zoos may not be able to keep up with the rate of decline in the wild. The harpy eagle is the kind of bird that could easily disappear in tropical American forests with no witnessed single event to mark the time when it happens.

The harpy eagle is awesome when it is seen in zoos and, for that reason, has been a desirable zoo specimen. With the threat to tropical rain forests as great as it is, the world's zoos are going to have to view this great bird in an increasingly urgent light. Far more attention is going to have to be paid to captive breeding, although it will probably be a very long time before any harpy eagles can be placed back in the wild with confidence. There would be little point in placing this bird in an area where the trees are all doomed to fall because they will take with them everything the harpy eagle needs.

198

# Bog Turtle

## CLEMMYS MUHLENBERGII

The pretty little bog turtle *(Clemmys muhlenbergii)*, once known as Muhlenberg's turtle, is one of those silent, cryptic animals that lives its life largely in secret. It will probably vanish the same way unless careful attention is paid to its needs. With a carapace, or top shell, no more than four and a half inches long, it is our smallest land turtle, and with its range seriously impacted it is probably our rarest.

It once ranged throughout the eastern states wherever swamps and sphagnum bogs could be found. Bog turtles are easily identified. They have dark-brown to black carapaces and temporal marking of bright yellow, orange, or red-orange. In some specimens, perhaps more often in some locales than others, the limbs are washed in orange or red. The carapace may have a light making in a starburst pattern. The exact extent of the original range is more a matter of conjecture than hard, recorded fact. Now, though, they are discontinuous with only a few widely spread populations north of Maryland and equally widely dispersed safe populations from Virginia southward. There are three known localities in Georgia where they can still be found. In North Carolina, there are over fifty localized populations and in South Carolina, just two.

The fate the bog turtle has suffered has a familiar ring to it. These turtles have been taken by collectors, far more than they ever should have been, and their bogs and swamps have been encroached upon by a growing and ever more demanding human population. Their bogs have been drained and paved over. Parking lots, condominiums, and shopping malls now stand on what was once prime bog turtle habitat. Bogs that have been allowed to remain in place have often been polluted by industrial facilities, toxic waste disposal, agricultural chemicals from adjacent farmland, and simply by drainage from highways and parking facilities.

To the untutored eye, a swamp or bog may appear to be a wasteland or a dirty place, but it is neither. A healthy swamp has a clean smell, clear water in most cases, and an enormous diversity of living plants and animals. The pH factor is constant (at least mildly acidic) and impure chemicals deleterious to living creatures do not appear unless man intrudes. Filthy, oily tires, cans, and containers that held all kinds of chemicals, insecticides, car batteries, outmoded machinery loaded with hydrocarbons, all of that human detritus is deadly and the bog turtles along with an unknowable number of other creatures have had to retreat. In most cases they simply stopped reproducing, mostly because they were unable to.

Fortunately zoos and the private collections of truly knowledgeable herpetologists have stepped in and bog turtles are being raised successfully in captivity. The zoo in Atlanta, for instance, has had bog turtles since 1967 and has been breeding them since 1974. At least one of the pairs there has lived for close to twenty years. The zoo has been releasing captive-hatched young into the same bogs where their parents came from. A permit is required for these animals to be held in captivity, and the kind of work being done by zoos and advanced and licensed amateurs should not be attempted by even the most well-meaning private individuals. No more pressure on wild stock should be permitted.

In captivity, the turtles are safe from predation so there is a higher egg-to-adult survival rate. In the wild, raccoons, skunks, and foxes are known to prey on eggs and the turtles themselves, particularly the young. Snapping turtles, water snakes, and large wading birds probably also take a toll. "Plinkers" out for a little harmless fun with their twenty-twos have been known to shoot them. Feral dogs and cats also kill some. When bog turtles have tried to find a new area that was less crowded or less polluted than their old spot, they have often encountered roads to cross. Not all drivers are concerned about turtles in the road, any more than they are about snakes.

Not all our wildlife is large and spectacular. Some of it is quiet and unobtrusive. Each species, though, is a cog in an amazing machine—life on earth. It is very important that zoos take on even the least-seeming of these. Although there is an essential element of showmanship that zoos must engage in to "build the gate," they seem to come into their own and prove their worth when they take on projects involving species with almost no sex appeal.

# San Francisco Garter Snake

## THAMNOPHIS SIRTALIS TETRATAENIA

One of the most exquisitely marked and colored of all North American reptiles is also one of the most seriously endangered snakes in the world. It is almost too much to hope that the splendid San Francisco garter snake *(Thamnophis sirtalis tetrataenia)* can long survive in the wild because its wild habitat is being taken away from it.

This, the most beautiful of all garter snakes, probably never had a range that extended beyond two counties, San Mateo and San Francisco. Specimens still exist, it is believed, or at least hoped, in the western part of San Francisco peninsula from San Francisco County into San Mateo about as far as Crystal Lake. It is impossible to estimate their numbers because they are, like all snakes, cryptic, shy, and seldom seen except by the most persistent and expert herpetologists.

Their young are born alive, about twenty-four to a clutch or litter, so if they had space and protection they could possibly multiply fairly rapidly. The mortality of the young, however, is not known, but cats, dogs, birds, and rats may keep a very large percentage from ever maturing.

But all of that is apparently academic. These snakes are not being left alone. Far from it. A large part of their known original range is already under concrete. Roads, housing developments, and other works of man generally have meant disaster for the subspecies. The control of water flow and the destruction of vegetation has meant further reduction in the areas where they can live. Some, certainly, die on the roads where they are likely to crawl on cool evenings to absorb the slowly dispersing heat of asphalt or concrete. Housing developments mean pets and children, and neither are healthy for a small, inoffensive snake with absolutely no means of protecting itself except by hiding. As areas are cleared for development and stripped of plant growth and natural rock

formations that could contain hiding places, these snakes are denied even that one opportunity to protect themselves. Like all snakes, exposed they die. The subspecies is simply giving ground, more each year, and the day may come in the not very distant future when the last specimen in the wild is stoned to death by children or crushed by a car. No one will ever be able to mark that day for only after many years of searching will the form be officially listed as "probably extinct in the wild."

There are very few San Francisco garter snakes in captivity. The photo of these specimens in the Sacramento Zoo shows that they can live under man's protection and in fact their reproductive potential is probably quite good. That will require our zoos to take more specimens from the wild and put their best reptile curators to work creating captive habitats suitable for the species. It will be, in the end, in all likelihood, the only solution. If it works, it may be possible in some future time to release specimens in protected areas that resemble their original habitat. There will be time enough to think about that later. The problem is to keep as many of the handsome little animals alive as possible.

Snakes as individuals and as species are fragile. As individuals they usually don't survive injuries. A stone thrown at a snake may drive the snake into protective cover but it may also cause an injury that will end with a fatal infection. Their bones, too, of course, are very small and fragile. As species snakes are often severely restricted in the habitat they can utilize. Their prey is often specific and limiting, and the temperature range they can tolerate is also. They must have cover or it is soon over. It is constant brinksmanship, a very hazardous existence even for venomous snakes, much less for harmless varieties such as garter snakes. The San Francisco garter snake is at this moment at the brink.

# Aruba Island Rattlesnake

## CROTALUS UNICOLORI

If there is one group of animals it is hard to gain sympathy for in this world, it is the rattlesnakes. They are an amazingly diverse group with between sixty-five and seventy different forms. They range from extreme southern Canada to deep down into tropical South America. They range in size from barely a foot to giants such as the Mexican west coast rattlesnake, at close to ten feet. The South American tropical rattler reaches eight and nine feet.

The severity of a rattlesnake's bite is a matter of considerable diversity. Most of these snakes have venom that is essentially hemotoxic, a blood poison; whereas the very dangerously venomous Mojave rattlesnake's venom is basically neurotoxic, like that of the cobras and mambas and kin.

No rattlesnake has a bite that is inevitably fatal, despite all the stories to the contrary. No rattlesnake has a bite that is quickly fatal except under the most unlikely circumstances. If a very large snake, for example, an eastern diamondback six or seven feet long, were to strike someone in the wrist and hit a major blood vessel, or in the face or throat, there would be dire consequences with a sudden onset. That would be a very unusual case, however. Most bites are on the extremities.

Rattlesnakes are not aggressive. They do not attack people or follow people or seek revenge on people. Those are all old wive's tales. Rattlesnakes are shy, retiring, and will stand their ground only when there is no alternative. They will not move toward trouble. At least a quarter of all rattlesnake bites are dry, that is, no venom is injected. In cases when venom is injected, it will most often be a sublethal dose.

Rattlesnakes are persecuted everywhere they are found. It is a rare backyard or farm they can hunt on or even pass through without being killed when seen. Cars and trucks swerve to run over them when they cross roads or seek the slowly dispersing heat of a paved surface on a cool night. All hands, literally, are turned against them, which is foolish and shortsighted, to say the least. Rats and mice, rattlesnake food, hurt and kill many more human beings every year than rattlesnakes do.

One rattlesnake in serious trouble is the smallish Aruba Island rattlesnake *(Crotalus unicolori).* The area it inhabits on its small island is only ten miles off the coast of Venezuela from whence it undoubtedly came long ago to evolve into a distinct species. It is the only one usually without a real rattle on its tail. Since tourism is the major industry of the island, development has taken much of the serpent's space. All that exist in the wild do so within a few square miles. The species, clearly, is endangered.

A number of zoos, particularly in North America, maintain Aruba Island rattlesnakes in their collections. More and more zoos are reporting success breeding the species. The Houston Zoo, particularly, has taken the Aruba Island rattlesnake on as a project, and although there are no plans now to release any back onto Aruba where the species evolved, there will eventually be a good captive reserve, to what end no one can say at this time. Still, captive breeding populations well dispersed is far better than unheralded extinction in the wild. The genetics of this interesting little animal will have been saved. Perhaps wiser men and women that we will know what that really means.

There may in fact be dimensions and purpose to the preservation of genetic material that is unique to each species, of course. Even if we cannot write the whole story now, zoo people and scientists in general seem to know by instinct that losing any species of plant or animal is wrong. At least for an animal like a rattlesnake, a zoo habitat can be humane. It doesn't suffer from confined space as larger, more intelligent animals do. It is a species that can be perserved without any hardship for the individuals selected to carry their genetic material forward.

# Photographers

**RON AUSTING**

Bali mynah, 145; Golden monkey, 101; Guam rail, 141; Cheetah, 5; Micronesian kingfisher 139; Parson's chameleon, 73

**TOM CAJACOB**

Beluga whale, 173; Siberian tiger, 97; Snow monkey, 99; Trumpeter swan, 187

**ROGER CARAS**

Nubian ibex, 21

**PHILLIP COFFEY**

Asian elephant, 107; Babirusa, 77; Caracal, 7; Cereopsis goose, 137; Cotton-top tamarin, 159; Giant panda, 103; Grevy zebra, 47; Indian rhinoceros, 123; Laysan duck, 195; Maned wolf, 183; Margay, 179; Mountain tapir, 177; Numbat, 133; Pink pigeon, 65; Pygmy hippo, 45; Radiated Tortoise, 71; Red panda, 105; Red-breasted goose, 135; San Francisco garter snake, 203; Sika deer, 113; Striped hyena, 49; Waldrapp ibis, 67; Wisent, 115

**JESSIE COHEN**

Barbery ape, 41; Spectacled bear, 185

**KATHERINE FENG**

Black rhinoceros, 35; Cougar, 167; Orangutan, 131; Snow leopard, 95; Spotted leopard, 3; Suricate, 15; White rhinoceros, 55

**RON GARRISON**

Malayan tapir, 121; Przewalski horse, 79; Szechwan takin, 87

**DAVID HARING**

Aye-Aye, 43; Bornean tarsier, 129; Philippine tarsier, 89; Ring-tailed lemur, 11; Sifaka, 9

**DENNIS W. HERMAN**

Bog turtle, 201

**BILL LOFTON**

Grizzly bear, 161; White-handed gibbon, 91

**CAROL LOFTON**

Asiatic lion, 109; Klipspringer, 25; Saddlebill stork, 63; San Joaquin kit fox, 165; Siamang, 93

**KENNETH LOVE**

Polar bear, 171

**TAD MOTOYAMA**

Aruba Island rattlesnake, 205; Bengal tiger, 111; Black leopard, 3; California condor, 191; Drill, 17; Eland, 27; Gaur, 117; Golden-headed tamarin, 155; Giant anteater, 181; Lowland gorilla, 53; North American bison, 163; Pangolin, 69; Red-eared guenon, 31; Red wolf, 169; Thick-billed parrot, 193; Zebra duiker, 37

**EVAN PELLER**

Asian small-clawed otter, 125; Giraffe, 13; Gray wolf, 175; Harpy eagle, 199; Koala bear, 127; Patas monkey, 29; Red uakari, 157; White Bengal tiger, 111

# Zoos and Institutions with Captive Wildlife

APPLE VALLEY ZOO, MINNESOTA
Beluga whale, 173; Siberian tiger, 97; Snow monkey, 99; Trumpeter swan, 187

AUDUBON PARK, NEW ORLEANS, LOUISIANA
Siamang, 93

CHESTER ZOO, ENGLAND
Asian elephant, 107

CHEYENNE MOUNTAIN ZOO, COLORADO
Grizzly bear, 161

CINCINNATI ZOO, OHIO
Bali mynah, 145; Cheetah, 5; Golden monkey, 101; Guam rail, 141; Micronesian kingfisher, 139; Parson's chameleon, 73

COLOGNE ZOOLOGICAL PARK, WEST GERMANY
Maned wolf, 183

DUKE UNIVERSITY CENTER FOR THE STUDY OF PRIMATE BIOLOGY AND HISTORY, NORTH CAROLINA
Aye-Aye, 43; Bornean tarsier, 129; Phillipine tarsier, 89; Ring-tailed lemur, 11; Sifaka, 9

EDINBURGH ZOO, SCOTLAND
Pygmy hippopotamus, 45

FRANKFURT ZOO, WEST GERMANY
Caracal, 7

FRESNO ZOO, CALIFORNIA
San Joaquin kit fox, 165

GLADYS PORTER ZOO, BROWNSVILLE, TEXAS
African elephant, 33

HAI-BAR NATURE RESERVES AUTHORITY, ISRAEL
Cypress wild sheep, 83; Dorcas gazelle, 61; Fallow deer, 119; Nubian ibex, 21; Scimitar-horned oryx, 57; Somali wild ass, 59

INTERNATIONAL CRANE FOUNDATION, BARABOO, WISCONSIN
Siberian crane, 143; Whooping crane, 189

JERSEY WILDLIFE PRESERVATION TRUST, ENGLAND
Babirusa, 77; Cereopsis goose, 137; Cotton-top tamarin, 159; Indian rhinoceros, 123; Laysan duck, 195; Numbat, 133; Pink pigeon, 65; Radiated tortoise, 71; Red-breasted goose, 135; San Francisco garter snake, 203; Waldrapp ibis, 67

LONDON ZOO, ENGLAND
Margay, 179

LOS ANGELES ZOO, CALIFORNIA
Aruba Island rattlesnake, 205; Asian small-clawed otter, 125; Bengal tiger, 111; Black rhinoceros, 35; California condor, 191; Cougar, 167; Drill, 17; Eland, 27; Gaur, 117; Giant anteater, 181; Giraffe, 13; Golden-headed tamarin, 155; Gray wolf, 175; Harpy eagle, 199; Koala bear, 127; Leopard, black and spotted, 3; Lowland gorilla, 53; North American bison, 163; Orangutan, 131; Pangolin, 69; Patas monkey, 29; Red-eared guenon, 31; Red uakari, 157; Red wolf, 169; Saddlebilled stork, 63; Snow leopard, 95; Suricate, 15; Thick-billed parrot, 193; White Bengal tiger, 111; White rhinoceros, 55; Zebra duiker, 37

MARWELL ZOOLOGICAL GARDEN, ENGLAND
Grevy zebra, 47; Sika deer, 113

MERU PARK, KENYA
White rhinoceros, 55

NATIONAL ZOOLOGICAL PARK, SMITHSONIAN INSTITUTION, WASHINGTON, D.C.
Barbery ape, 41; Spectacled bear, 185

NATIONAL ZOO, DELHI, INDIA
Indian rhinoceros, 123

NEW YORK ZOOLOGICAL SOCIETY, NEW YORK
Père David's deer, 81

NORTH CAROLINA ZOOLOGICAL PARK
Chimpanzee, 51

ROGER WILLIAMS PARK ZOO, PROVIDENCE, RHODE ISLAND
Polar bear, 171

SACRAMENTO ZOO, CALIFORNIA
Asiatic lion, 109

SAN ANTONIO ZOO, TEXAS
Klipspringer, 25

# Index of Animals